THE BOOK OF

JUBILEES

Translated from the Ethiopic

by

REV. GEORGE H. SCHODDE, Ph.D.
Professor in Capital University, Columbus, Ohio

A REPRINT FROM AN EDITION PUBLISHED

by

E. J. GOODRICH

OBERLIN, OHIO

1888

PUBLISHER

ARTISAN PUBLISHERS
P.O. Box 1529
Muskogee, Oklahoma 74402
(918) 682-8341
www.artisanpublishers.com

ISBN 0-934666-07-5
Library of Congress catalog card number: 80-53467

1

THE FORMATION OF EVE

One of the most marked features of theological research in our day and decade is the intense interest which characterizes the work in biblical theology, technically so called, and in this department no auxiliary branch has been more productive of good results than has been that discipline called History of New Testament Times, or the study of the times of Christ as to their religious, moral, and social features. The aim of such study is to reproduce, as far as possible, the exact picture of Christ's earthly career in the midst of all the agencies which influenced him and upon which he exerted his influence; in other words, to understand Christ's words and works with their true historical background and surroundings. It is a line of investigation that has produced, indirectly, such masterpieces as Weber's **System der altsynagogalen palastinischen Theologie** (Leipzig, 1880), and, directly, such as Edersheim's Life and Times of Jesus the Messiah, as also the two **Neu-Testamentliche Zeitgeschichten**, of Schurer and Hausrath, as well as many other works, smaller in dimensions and more closely circumscribed in scope, while the spirit and method of this research is felt in every fibre of the leading exegetical and historical works on biblical subjects. The object of all this study is to produce an accurate and truly historical picture of Christ and Christianity.

In the pursuit of this aim the Book of Jubilees has a not unimportant mission. This importance lies in the fact that it, if carefully studied, will furnish valuable contributions toward the understanding of that problem which lies back and behind all the work and teachings of both Christ and his disciples, as also of the writings of the latter, namely, the doctrines, beliefs, and spirit of New Testament Judaism. Christ came unto his own, and his own received him not (John i. 11), because Israel had departed from the revelations of God. Instead of a justification by faith, as is taught throughout the whole Old Testament, the contemporaries of our Lord taught a justification by the law, a legal righteousness. The central principle of Jewish orthodoxy was the nomistic principle, that obedience to the law in all its real and imagined ramifications must be the basis of acceptance before God. Thus there was an impassable gulf fixed between the theological system of the Jews and that of Christ and his disciples. The latter was a further development from Old Testament premises; the former was a radical departure from all pre-Christian revelation. This woeful heterodoxy, which constituted the backbone and marrow of the accepted theology of the day, meets Christ and his disciples wherever they work or speak, and has been an all-powerful factor in moulding the shape and form which the New Testament revelation and development has assumed. We need in this connection to cite as examples

3

only the Pauline doctrine of the law, in which he antagonizes, not the law as such, but only the false stand-point of the Jews in regard to the law, and his outspoken and decided championship of the doctrine of justification by faith alone over against a justification by works, suggested, beyond all doubt, by the fundamental error of the Jewish system of his day.

In the study of these problems the book before us finds its mission. The editor of the Ethiopic text and German translator, Professor Dillmann, has proved to the satisfaction of scholars in general, that the book is a production of the first Christian century. In Ewald's **Jahrbucher der biblischen Wissenschaft** for 1850 and 1851, he has published a German translation of the book from a single and defective manuscript, and added a short discussion of the contents. There (pp. 90-4) he shows that the book presupposes and cites those parts of the Book of Enoch which date up to about the birth of Christ, while it, in turn, has been used and quoted by the Testament of the Twelve Patriarchs, a work similar in spirit and a product of the early part of the second century. This will decide the end of the first century after Christ as the date for the composition of the Book of Jubilees. By Christian authors the work is not quoted until later. Epiphanius, Jerome, and Rufinus are the first to mention it, while Syncellus, Cedrinus, and other Byzantine writers quote from it at length. These citations are collected in Fabricius, **Codex Pseudepigraphus Veteris Testamenti**, 1722, vol. i. pp. 849-64. But the testimony of the **Testamentum XII. Patriarcharum** is decisive as to the **terminus ad quem**. Ronsch, who has made a most exhaustive study of the book, confidently claims that it was written before the destruction of the temple, pointing to the words in c. 1, 23; 49, 27, and similar passages, which could not have been written after that event. Cf. also Drummond, The Jewish Messiah, p. 146, and Schurer, 1. c. 463.

As the book is undoubtedly the work of a Palestinian Jew and written in Hebrew (although the Ethiopic is translated from the Greek — cf. Dillmann, 1. c. p. 88 ff.), it can be fairly considered as an outgrowth of that school and spirit of Judaism which we in the New Testament find arrayed in opposition to Christianity and its work. The book can best be described by calling it a haggadic commentary on certain portions of Genesis and the opening chapters of Exodus, and it is thus the oldest of all the Midrashim, and a representative example of the manner in which the learned contemporaries of Christ made use of the biblical books for their own peculiar purpose and object. It is a sample of an exegetical Targum of those days in the spirit of New Testament Judaism. Just to what particular school of Jewish thought it owes its origin would be difficult to decide. Since the publication of the German translation, a number of Jewish scholars, such as Jellenek (**Beth-ha-Midrash**, 1855, p. x. ff.), Beer (**Das Buch der Jubilaen**, 1856), Frankel (**Monatsschrift fur Geschichte u. Wissen-**

4

schaft des Judenthums, 1856), and earlier, Treuenfels (**Literaturblatt des Orients**, p. 1846), have discussed the problem, one advocating a Samaritan origin, another an Essene, another claiming that it arose in the Egyptian Diaspora, but all agreeing as to its thoroughly Jewish origin and, in general, its representative character, while Ronsch even thinks that he detects an anti-Christian tendency (**Das Buch der Jubilaen, oder die kleine Genesis**, pp. 518-20).

What time and source would indicate is amply verified by an examination of the contents. This, of course, cannot be the place, nor is it our object, to analyze critically the contents of the book, but by pointing to a few prominent features it will be readily seen how thoroughly the book harmonizes with the leading thoughts of Jewish orthodoxy in Christ's day. The centre of that orthodoxy was the law, and its paraphernalia, and all means, lawful and unlawful, were put into requisition to exalt the importance of that law and to increase its authority. The eternity and pre-existence of this law, its festivals and its ceremonies, are accepted beliefs of later Judaism (cf. Weber, 1. c. & 4 ff.). To the service of this dogma the writer of the book of Jubilees has lent his pen. He again and again maintains the thesis that the law existed from eternity, although revealed in full only through Moses; that even in heaven, before the creation, the angels observed the festivals, services, and ceremonies of this law; that throughout their lives the patriarchs all strictly carried out its behests. All these things were written on the "tablets of heaven," and were gradually introduced among the pious fathers as occasion offered an opportunity, and the teachings concerning them were laid down in writing at the very beginning, which books of mystery were handed down from father to son in theocratic succession. This is the leading thought of the whole work, and, in some form or other, is found in nearly every chapter. It is a remarkable example of how willing the Jews in Christ's day were to emply a most remarkable exegesis in order to make the records of revelation accord with their false view of its legal features.

Besides this leading characteristic of the work, there are many others of less importance that are interesting and instructive, and that cast a discerning light on the Jewish world of thought at the New Testament era. Outwardly the leading feature is the chronological system of the book, namely, its division of all ancient history of the Israelites according to the sacred periods of jubilees of forty-nine years, which fact gives it one of its Greek names, Τὰ 'Ιωβηλαῖα (Epiphanius, **adv. Her.**, 1, 3, 6), the other being ἡ λεπτὴ γένεσις, λεπτογένεσις, or μικρογένεσιϲ, so called, not because it is shorter than the canonical Genesis, but because it had less authority. The time between the creation and the entrance of Israel into Canaan is counted as fifty jubilees, or 2,450 years, which in general agrees with the biblical records. In the details of this chronological arrangement there are the occasionally slight variations from the Hebrew text, and in these instances there is often a surprising agreement with the Septuagint and the Samaritan versions. Dillmann is probably correct (p. 77) in ascribing these variations from the Hebrew, not to the author, but to the translator, accomodating the numbers to the Septuagint text recognized among the Greeks.

It is remarkable how the writer bridges over all the difficulties of the canonical Genesis. The speaking of the serpent in Paradise is explained by the fact that before the fall all animals could speak; he knows the names of all the wives of the patriarchs, also the day and month when their children were born; he shows how Genesis II. 17 was literally fulfilled, since before the Lord a thousand years are as one day, and Adam died before he was a thousand years old; a parallel exegesis to this is found in Justin Martyr c. Tryphone 81. He narrates with whose assistance Noah brought the animals into the ark; how the Hamitic tribes of Palestine unlawfully took possession of Shem's portion; that Rebecca loved Jacob more than Esau because Abraham had told her that the younger son would be the theocratic successor; also why it was that Amnon refused to take Tamar to wife; how Moses was preserved in the bulrushes, etc., and many other biblical narratives are explained and complemented in various manners, usually in an apologetical spirit.

The book is also full of stories and fables concerning the fathers in Israel, some of these being found also in the Testament of the Twelve Patriarchs, and other earlier and later works, but many not preserved elsewhere. In this connection we mention the names of the wives of the patriarchs and of the sons of Jacob; the name of the land to which Adam was driven after the expulsion from Eden; the number of the sons of Adam; the four sacred mountains of the earth; the name of the mountain of the Ararat chain where the ark rested; the extensive account of the fall of the angels in the days of Jared, together with the dire consequences of their sins with the daughters of men, which story forms the burden of the earliest portions of this book; the story of the books of Enoch, Noah, Abraham, Isaac, and others; the early days of Abraham, his piety, and fight against the idolatry of his father's house; the ten temptations of Abraham, and many similar stories concerning Jacob and his relations to Esau, and concerning the sons of Jacob and their history. The angelology and demonology of the book are carried out quite extensively, and in the main thoughts agree with the ideas found in other apocalyptic works. The patriarchs are all models of virtue, and especially prominent through their observance of the Levitical ordinances and ceremonies. The rest of the work is in harmony with these statements. Bot through what it states and what it omits, the work is instructive in teaching what was the **Zeitgeist** among the Jews in those memorable days.

But, of course, the full contribution of the Book of Jubilees to the

New Testament can only be secured through a careful and patient study of every chapter and verse. In order to enable scholars who are not acquaintd with the Ethiopic to do this work, the present translation is here offered. It has been made directly from the best Ethiopic text accessible, and with the best aids at the translator's command. As has been stated above, the German translation by Dillmann is from a single defective and poor manuscript. Nine years after its publication, in 1859, Dillmann, the prince of Ethiopic scholars in our century, issued a critical edition of the Ethiopic text on the basis of two manuscripts, entitled, **Liber Jubilacorum Qui idem a Graccis 'H** λεπτὴ γένεσις **inscribitur, versione Graeca deperdita, nunc nonnisi in Geez lingua conservatus, nuper ex Abyssinia in Europam allatus, Aethiopice ad duorum librorum manuscriptorum fidem primum edidit Dr. August Dillmann**. He had hoped himself to make a new translation of the book from this improved text (cf. Praefatio p. x.), but has never been able to do so. In Ronsch's edition, however, of a Latin fragment of the book found in 1861 by Ceriani, and embracing about one-third of the book, he has given a Latin translation from the Ethiopic of those sections corresponding to the Ceriani fragment. The need of a new translation has frequently been urged (cf. **e. g.**, Drummond, 1. c., p. 144). As there is no such version in any modern language, the present translator has attempted to do this, leaving to others to investigate the book in its whole length, depth, and breadth. In order to facilitate the study of the book, the translator has not only adopted the division of Dillmann into chapters, but has also divided these again into verses. The lack of this latter feature in Dillmann makes the use of his version very difficult. The fullest discussion of the book is that of Ronsch, besides whose work those mentioned in this introductory note may be consulted. The English reader will find valuable aid in Drummond, pp. 143-147.

These are the words of the division* of days, according to the law and testimony,** according to the events of the years, according to their sevens, according to their Jubilees, to all the years of the world, according to the word of the Lord on Mount Sinai to Moses, when he ascended to receive the stone tablets of the law and the commandments by the voice of the Lord when he said to him: "Ascend to the top of the mountain!"†

CHAP. I. And it happened in the first year of the exodus of the children of Israel out of Egypt, in the 3rd month, on the 16th of this month, and the Lord spoke to Moses saying: "Ascend to me here on the mountain, and I will give to thee the two stone tablets of the law and the commandments; as I have written them, thou shalt make them known." 2. And Moses ascended the mountain of the Lord, and the glory of the Lord dwelt on the mountain of Sinai, and a cloud overshadowed it six days. 3. And the Lord called to Moses on the seventh day in the midst of the cloud; and he saw the glory of the Lord like a flaming fire on the top of the mountain. ‡ 4. And Moses was there on the mountain forty days and forty nights, and the Lord instructed him in regard to what was past and what would be, the words of the division of days, both in the law and the testimony. 5. And he said to him: "Incline thy heart to every word which I shall speak to thee, and write them into a book, in order that their generations may see how I have left them on account of all the evil which they do, in rebelling and in deserting the covenant which I established between me and thee this day on Mount Sinai for their generations. 6. And it will be and these words shall declare it thus when all the punishments shall come over them; and they will know that I am more righteous than they in all their judgments and their desires, and they will know that I was with them. 7. And thou, write for thyself all these words which I make known to thee this day (for I know their rebellion and their stiff

---

* Kufale, i. e., division, or rather, "Book of Division," is the name by which this book is known among the Abyssinians. As such it is cited, e.g., in the Apolostic Canons, 55. In Fell's edition, c. 56, we read of "three books of the Kufale." The name is derived from the fact that the author divides the history he records according to the chronological system of jubilee periods.

** Both words used in the original for law and testimony are frequently employed for "covenant," διαϑήκη. The two together evidently express the covenant relation between Israel and Jehovah.

† In claiming divine and Sinaitic authority for the production before us, the author does nothing more than what is claimed for the whole of the oral traditions of the Jews. Cf. especially the opening sentences of the **Pirke Aboth** in the Mishna. The apocalypses of the same period also claim inspiration, prominently the book of Enoch. Such a **pia fraus** was manifestly not considered a moral wrong.

‡ Cf. Ex. xxiv. 15-17.

neck *) before I shall lead them into the land which I have sworn to their fathers, to Abraham and Isaac and to Jacob, saying, "To your seed I will give this land, which flows with milk and honey; and they shall eat and be satisfied. 8. And they will turn themselves to false gods, who did not deliver them from all their oppression; and this testimony will be heard against them for a testimony. 9. For they will forget all my ordinances which I have commanded them, and will walk after the Gentiles and after their impurity and after their shame, and will serve their gods, and these will become for them an offence unto oppression and misfortune and for a trap. 10. And many will be destroyed and will be taken captive and will fall into the hands of the enemy, because they have deserted my ordinances and my commands and the festivals of my covenant, and my sabbaths and that which I have sanctified to myself in their midst, and my tabernacle and my sanctuary which I have sanctified to myself in the midst of the land that I should set my name over it and it should dwell there. 11. And they will make to themselves altars on heights and groves and sculptured idols, and each one will worship his own idol for sin, and they will offer their children to the demons and to all the deeds of the error of their hearts. 12. And I will send witnesses to them that I may testify over them, but they will not hear and will slay my witnesses, and they will cast out those who seek the law, and will abolish the whole (law), and will begin to do evil before my eyes. 13. And I will hide my face from them and I will deliver them over to the Gentiles for captivity and for binding and for devouring and for expelling them from the midst of the land, and I shall scatter them in the midst of the Gentiles. 14. And they will forget all my law and all my commandments and all my judgment, and they will err in reference to new moons and sabbaths and festivals and jubilees and ordinances. 15. And then they will turn themselves to me from the midst of the Gentiles with all their hearts and all their soul and all their power, and I shall gather them from amongst all the Gentiles, and they will seek me that I may be found for them when they seek me with all their heart and with all their soul, and I will open to them much peace and righteousness. 16. And I will transplant them as a plant of righteousness, with all my heart and with all my soul, and they will be to me for a blessing and not for a curse, a head and not a tail; and I will build up my sanctuary in their midst, and I will dwell with them, and I will be to them their God, and they shall be to me my people, in truth and in righteousness, and I will not desert them and will not deny them, for I am the Lord their God." 17. And Moses fell down upon his face, and he prayed and said: "My Lord and my God, do not forsake thy people and thy inheritance to wander in the error of their hearts, and do not

---

* Deut. xxxi. 27. Here, and indeed throughout the opening chapters of the book, there is a marked similarity between the author's ideas and that of the book of Deuteronomy.

deliver them into the hands of their enemies, the Gentiles, that these may not rule over them, and that they do not make them to sin against thee. 18. O Lord, let thy mercy be raised over thy people, and create for them a righteous mind, and let not the spirit of Beliar* rule over them to accuse them before thee, to entrap them away from the path of righteousness, that they be destroyed from before thy face. 19. But they are thy people and thy inheritance, which thou hast delivered from the hands of the Egyptians with thy great power; and create in them a clean heart and a holy spirit, and let them not be entrapped in their sins from now on and to eternity!" 20. And the Lord said to Moses: "I know their contrariness and their thoughts and their stiff neck, and they will not obey until they learn their sins and the sins of their fathers. And after this they will turn to me in all righteousness and with their whole heart and with their whole soul, and I will circumcise the foreskin of their hearts and the foreskin of the hearts of their seed, and I will create for them a holy spirit, and will cleanse them so that they do not turn away from me from this day to eternity. 21. And their souls will cling to me and to all my commandments, and my commandments shall return to them, and I will be to them a father, and they shall be to me children. And they shall all be called the children of the living God, and will know all things of the spirit and all things of service, and it will be known that they are my children and that I am their father in righteousness and in truth, and that I love them. 22. And thou, write down for thyself all these words which I have this day made known to thee on this mountain, the first and the last and what is future, according to all the division of days in the law and in the testimony, and according to the weeks ** of the jubilees to eternity, until I descend and dwell with them in all eternity." 23. And he said to the angel of the face: † "Write for Moses from the beginning of creation until my sanctuary shall have been established in their midst for all eternity, and the Lord will have appeared to the eyes of all, and all will know that I am the God of Israel and the Father of all of the children of Jacob and King on Mount

* Beliar, βελίαρ , cf. 2 Cor. vi. 15, a name of Satan frequently found in apocalyptic and early ecclesiastical literature.

** The word "weeks" is used throughout the work in the sense of week of years, i. e., forty-nine years, or one jubilee period.

† The biblical מלאך הפנים, favorite angels of apocalyptic writers, whose mission is the mediatorship between God and man. Later writers resort to this means of communication between divinity and humanity all the more in order to preserve the former from all contact with the latter, and thus preserve the holiness of God. The idea is born from the same spirit that induced the Septuagint translators to smooth over the anthropomorphism and anthropopathies of the Hebrew text, and helped much to the development of Philo's **logos** idea and allegorical method of interpretation, as also to the popularity of the **Memre** mediatorship in God's dealings with men and the world so generally prevalent in the Targumim. Cf. Zech. i. 9, and similar passages, and also Weber, System der altsynag. palest. Theologie, passim.

Zion from eternity to eternity. And Zion and Jerusalem will be holy." 24. And the angel of the face, who went before the tents of Israel, took the tablets of the division of years from the time of creation, the law and the testimony for the weeks and the jubilees, each year according to all its number and the jubilees according to years from the day of the new creation, when heaven and earth were created new, and also all creation according to the powers of heaven and all the creation of the earth, until then when the sanctuary of the Lord will be made in Jerusalem on Mount Zion, and all the luminaries will be renewed for a healing and for peace and for a blessing for all the chosen of Israel, that it may be thus from this day on and to all the days of the world!

CHAP. II. And the angel of the face spoke to Moses by the command of the Lord, saying: "Write all the words of creation, how in six days the Lord God finished all the works which he created, and rested on the seventh day and sanctified it for all the years and established it as a sign for all his works." For on the first day he created the heavens above and the earth and the waters and all the spirits that serve before him, and the angels of the face and the angels that cry "holy," and the angels of the spirit of fire,* and the angels of the spirit of wind, and the angels of the spirit of the clouds of darkness and of hail and of hoarfrost, and the angels of the abysses and of thunder and of lightning, and the angels of the spirits of cold and of heat, of winter and of spring and of fall and of summer and of all the spirits of the multitude of works which are in the heavens and on the earth and in all the depths, and of darkness and of light and of dawn and of eve which he has prepared in the knowledge of his heart. 2. And at that time we saw his work and praised him and lauded before him on account of all his work, for seven great things did he make on the first day.** 3. And on the second day he made a firmament between the waters, and the waters divided on this day, and half of it ascended upward, and half of it descended beneath the firmament over the face of the earth. And this work alone was made on the second day. 4. And on the third day he did as he said to the waters that they should cross from the face of the whole earth to one place, and that dry land should appear. 5. And he made the waters thus as he said to them, and they gathered from over the face of the earth into one place outside of this firmament, and the dry land appeared. 6. And on that day he created for it (the water) the abysses of the seas, according to their separate gathering places, and all the rivers and the

---

* The idea underlying this and similar expressions found so frequently in the Jewish apocalypses is that all objects in nature which can be agencies for good or for evil are under the management of particular angels who direct their use according to the will of the Lord. Especially is this the case in the Noachic fragments of Enoch. Cf. the translator's version of that book (Andover, 1882), chap. 60 sqq. and notes.

** I. e., heaven, earth, water, serving spirits, angels of the face, angels of praise, and angels of the elements. Cf. also verse 17 of this chapter.

gathering places of the waters in the hills and in all the earth, and all the lakes, and all the dew of the earth, and the seed which is sown according to its kind, and every thing that is eaten, and the trees which bear fruit, and the wild trees, and the garden of Eden for pleasure; and all these four* great creations he made on the third day. 7. And on the fourth day he made the sun and moon and stars and placed them in the firmament of heaven that they should shine over the earth and to rule over day and night and to divide between night and day and between darkness and light. 8. And God established the sun as a great sign over the earth and for days and for sabbaths and for months and for festivals and for years and for jubilees and for all seasons of the years. 9. And he shall divide between light and darkness and for prosperity that all things that sprout and grow on earth may prosper. 10. These three kinds God made on the fourth day. 11. And on the fifth day he created the great animals in the abysses of the seas (for these were the first things of flesh created by his hands), and every thing that moves in the waters, and the fishes and every thing that flies, the birds and their whole kind. 12. And the sun arose over them to prosper them, and over all that was on th earth, every thing that sprouts out of the earth and all the trees that bear fruit and all flesh: these three kinds he made on the fifth day. 13. And on the sixth day he made all the animals of the earth and all the beasts and every things that moves over the earth. 14. And after all this he made mankind, a single one; male and female he created them, and made him ruler over all things upon the earth and in the seas and over that which flies and over all the animals and beasts and over every thing that moves on the earth, and over the whole earth; and over all this he made him ruler. 15. And these four kinds he made on the sixth day. And there were altogether twenty-two kinds.** 16. And he completed all his work on the sixth day, † all that is in the heavens and on the earth and in the seas and in the abysses, in the light and in the darkness and in every thing; and he gave us (the angels) a great sign, the day of sabbaths, that we should do work six days, and should rest on the sabbath from all work. 17. And all the angels of the face and all the angels that cry "holy," to us, these two great kinds, he said that we should observe the sabbath with him in heaven and on earth. ‡ 18. And he said to us: "Behold, I shall

* I. e., the terra firma, the gathering places for the water, the plants, and Eden.

** I. e., seven kinds on the first day, one on the second, four on the third, three on the fourth, three on the fifth, and four on the sixth day.

† The writer follows the Septuagint with its $\dot{\epsilon}\nu\ \tau\tilde{\eta}\ \dot{\eta}\mu\dot{\epsilon}\rho\alpha\ \tau\tilde{\eta}\ \dot{\epsilon}\kappa\tau\eta$ in Gen. ii.2. It will be remembered that the Hebrew text here has ביום השביעי.

‡ Not only the pre-existence of great persons, such as the Messiah, but of sacred objects and ceremonies is a favorite idea of apocalyptic writers. According to the book of Jubilees, the Israelite economy was but a reflex and reproduction of an eternal and more perfect **hierarchia caelestis** among the angels around the throne of grace. Cf. especially the translator's introduction to Enoch p. 48 sqq.

separate for myself a people from among all the nations, and these shall celebrate the sabbath, and I shall sanctify them unto myself as a nation, and I will sanctify them unto myself as a people, and will bless them, as I have sanctified the day of sabbaths, and I will sanctify them unto me and thus I will bless them; and they shall be to me my people, but I will be to them a God.   19. And I chose the seed of Jacob from among all that I have seen and have written him down as a first born son, and I have sanctified him unto myself forever and ever; and the day of the sabbaths I will teach them, that they observe sabbath on it from all work."   20. And he made therein a sign that they too should observe the sabbath with us on the seventh day, to eat and to drink and to bless him who has created all things, as he blessed and sanctified unto himself a people which shall appear from amongst the nations and that they should observe the sabbathtogether with us. And he caused that before him his commands should ascend like a sweet savor which should be acceptable before him all the days of the twenty-two heads of men from Adam to Jacob. And twenty-two kinds of works were made until this seventh day;* this thing is bless ed and holy, and the former too is blessed and holy and this one with that one serves for a sanctification and blessing.   21. And to this one (Jacob and his seed) was given that they should be for all the days the blessed and holy ones of the testimony and the first law, just as he had blessed and sanctified the seventh day on the seventh day.   22. He created heaven and earth and every thing that he created in six days, and the Lord established a holy festival day for all his creation; and therefore he commanded on its account that he who does any work on it shall die, and whoever defiles it shall surely die.   23. And thou, command the children of Israel, and they shall observe this day, so that they keep it holy and do not work on it any work, and do not defile it; for it is holier than all the days.   24. All who profane this day shall surely die, and all who do any work on it shall surely die forever; so that the children of Israel observe this day in their generations and be not rooted out of the land; for it is a holy day and a blessed day. 25. And every man who observe it and keeps the sabbath on it away from all his work, will be blessed and holy for all his days like unto me. 26. And announce and say to the children of Israel the law of this day, and that they shall observe the sabbath on it, and do not desert it in the error of their hearts, and that they be not engaged in doing any- thing on it which should not be done, and that they do not prepare on it any thing that is eaten or drunk, nor draw water, nor on it carry in or bring out of their gates any thing that is carried, which they have not prepared for themselves as a work on the six days in their houses.

* In connection with this observe, that as there had been twenty-two different works of creation before the sanctification of the sabbath by the angels (cf. v. 15 sqq.) thus too there should be twenty-two generations of people before in Israel a nation should arise that would establish the sanctification of the sabbath on earth.

27. And they shall not carry out or bring in on that day from one house to another, for this is a holy and blessed day over all the days of jubilees; on it we observed the sabbath in heaven, before it was known to any mortal to observe the sabbath on it on the earth. 28. And the Creator of all blessed it; but he did not sanctify all nations and peoples to observe the sabbath on it, only Israel alone: to them alone he granted to eat and to drink and to observe sabbath on it on the earth. 29. And the Creator of all blessed it, who had created this day for a blessing and a sanctification and for glory above all the days. 30. This law and testimony was given to the children of Israel as a law forever to their generations.

CHAP. III. 1. And in the sixth day of the second sabbath we brought, by the command of the Lord, to Adam all the animals and all the beasts and all the birds and every thing that moves on the earth and every thing that moves in the water, each according to their kind, and each according to their similarity: on the first day the animals; the beasts on the second day; the birds on the third day; every thing that moves on the earth the fourth day; whatever moves in the water on the fifth day. 2. And Adam gave unto each its name; and as he called them, this was their name. And on these five days Adam saw this: a male and a female in each kind that is on the earth, but that he was alone and could not find a companion who could be an aid to such as he. 3. And God said to me:* "It is not good that man should be alone: let us make for him a helpmeet like unto him." 4. And the Lord our God caused a stupor to fall upon him and he slept, and he took for a wife one rib from amongst his ribs, and this rib was made into a woman from amongst his ribs, and he built flesh there in its place, and build a woman. 5. And he awakened Adam out of his sleep, and awakening he arose on the sixth day and came to her and knew her and said unto her: 'This is now bone of my bone and flesh from my flesh: this one shall be called my wife, for she came and originated from man. 6. For this reason man and wife shall be one, and for this reason a man shall leave his father and his mother and will connect himself with his wife, and they shall be one flesh. 7. And in the first seventh was Adam created, and his wife in his side, and in the second seventh he showed her to him,** and on that account the command was given to observe in their defilement seven days for a male and twice seven days for a female. † 8. And when Adam had completed forty days in the land where he had been created, we brought him into the garden of Eden, that he should work it and watch it; but his wife they brought in on the eightieth day, and after this she entered the garden; and on this account the commandment is

* I. e., to the angel who is narrating these matters to Moses.

** I.e., she was created at the same time with Adam, but in and within him, and it was only in the second week that she became a separate creature.

† Cf. Lev. xii.

written on the tablets of heaven * in reference to her that gives birth, that "if she brings forth a male, she shall remain in her uncleanness seven days according to the first week of her days, and thirty days shall she abide in the blood of purifying, and she shall touch nothing holy and shall not enter into the sanctuary until these days are completed for her who has a male child. 9. But she who has a female child shall remain in her uncleanness two weeks, according to the first two weeks, and sixty-six days in the blood of purifying, and all the days for her shall be eighty." ** 10. And she having completed these eighty days we brought her into the garden of Eden, for it is holy above the whole earth, and every tree that is planted in it is holy. And on this account was ordained concerning her that gives birth to a male or female this law for these days, that they shall touch nothing holy nor enter a sanctuary until these days for a male or a female are completed. † 11. This law and testimony was given and written for the children of Israel that they should observe it all the days. 12. And in the first week of the first jubilee Adam and his wife were in the garden of Eden seven years working and watching it; and we gave them work and taught them to work every thing that offered itself for work. 13. And he labored and was naked and did not know it and was not ashamed, and he watched the garden against the birds and the animals and the beasts, ‡ and gathered its fruits and ate and laid aside the rest for himself and his wife, and laid aside that which he had guarded for himself. 14. And having ended the completion of seven years which he completed there, in the seventh year exactly, and in the second month, on the seventeenth day of the month, the serpent came and approached the woman, and the serpent said to the woman: "Has God commanded that you shall not eat of any of the fruit of the trees in the garden?" 15. And she said to it: "He has told us, ' Eat from all the fruit of the trees in the garden, but from the fruit of the tree which is in the midst of the garden ye shall not eat, nor shall ye touch it, that ye die not!'" 16. And the serpent said to the woman: "Ye will surely not die, but because God knows that on which day ye eat of it your eyes shall be opened and ye shall be like gods and will know good and evil." 17. And the woman saw the tree that it was pleasant and it pleased the eye, and that its fruit was good to eat; she took from it and ate. 18. And she first covered her shame with

* Throughout this and similar works the laws of God and his ordinances are looked upon as taken from the tablets of heaven; especially is this idea and expression found in the Testamentum XII. Patriarcharum.

** Cf. Lev. xv.

† To the present day yet this law is preserved in the Church of Abyssinia. Cf. Thiersch's elaborate articles on Abyssinia in the July and August numbers of the Allgm. Conservat. Monatschrift for 1884.

‡ On this point our book differs from other apocalypses where the animals before the fall are represented as harmless.

fig leaves, and gave to her husband, and he ate, and his eyes were opened and he saw that he was naked. 19. And he took fig leaves and sewed them together and made for himself an apron and covered his shame. 20. And God cursed the serpent and was enraged at it forever; and he was enraged at the woman also, because she had obeyed the voice of the serpent, and he said to her: "I shall surely increase thy pains and thy trouble; in thy pains bear children, and to thy husband be thy refuge, and he shall be thy lord." 21. And to Adam he said: "Because thou didst obey the voice of thy wife and didst eat from this tree of which I had commanded thee that thou shouldst not eat, let the earth be cursed on account of thy deed; thorns and thistles shall it bring forth for thee; and eat thou thy bread in the sweat of thy brow until thou returnest to the earth from which thou hast been taken; for earth thou art, and to earth thou shalt return." 22. And he made for them garments of skin and clothed them, and sent them from the garden. 23. And on that day on which Adam came out of the garden of Eden he offered, as a sweet savour, a burnt offering: frankincense and galbanum and myrrh spices, in the morning with the rising of the sun, on the day when he covered his shame. 24. And on that day was closed the mouth of all the animals and of the beasts and of the birds and of whatever walks and of whatever moves, so that they could not speak; for they all had spoken with each other one lip and one tongue.* 25. And he sent out of the garden of Eden all flesh that was in the garden of Eden, and all flesh was scattered according to its kinds and according to its natures to the places which had been created for them. 26. And to Adam alone did he give to cover his shame, of all the animals and beasts. 27. On this account it is commanded in the tablets of heaven concerning all who know the judgment of the law, that they shall cover their shame and shall not uncover themselves as the Gentiles uncover themselves. 28. And at the new moon of the fourth month Adam and his wife came out of the garden of Eden and dwelt in the land of Elda, in the land of their creation. 29. And Adam called the name of his wife Eve. 30. And they did not have a son until the first jubilee year; and after this he knew her. 31. But he cultivated the land, as he had been taught in the garden of Eden.

CHAP. IV. 1. And in the third week of the second jubilee she gave birth to Cain, and in the fourth she gave birth to Abel, and in the fifth she gave birth to her daughter Awan.** 2. And in the first (week)

---

* The idea that animals spoke before the fall is not confined to this book.

** Who invented this and the other non-biblical names that are found in this and the following chapters is not known. As in the whole known literature of that day and kind there is no other book that contains so many of them as does the one before us, it may not be incorrect to think that the author himself invented many. But he is certainly not the originator of the idea of inventing such names. Indications abound that the popular Hebrew faith of the day had many such names.

17

of the third jubilee Cain slew Abel, because (God) accepted an offering from his hands, but did not receive a fruit offering from the hands of Cain. 3. And he slew him on the field; and his blood cried aloud from earth to heaven lamenting that he had slain him, and God punished Cain, because he had slain Abel. 4. And he made him a refugee over the earth, on account of the blood of his brother, and he cursed him upon the earth. 5. And on this account it is written in the tablets of heaven: "Cursed be he who slays his neighbor in wickedness, and all who hear shall say, 'So be it!' and the man who sees it and does not announce it, cursed be he like the other." 6. And on this account we hearing come to announce before the Lord our God all the sins which take place in heaven and earth, and in light and in darkness, and everywhere. 7. And Adam and his wife mourned Abel four weeks of years; and in the fourth year of the fifth week he became joyful and knew his wife again, and she brought forth for him a son, and they called his name Seth; for he said: "The Lord has raised up for us a second seed on the earth in the place of Abel; for Cain slew him." 8. In the sixth week he begat his daughter Azura. 9. And Cain took Awan his sister to himself as wife, and she brought forth for him Enoch at the end of the fourth jubilee. nd in the first year of the first week of the fifth jubilee houses were built on the earth, and Cain built a city, and called it by the name of his son Enoch. 10. And Adam knew Eve, his wife, and she brought forth yet nine sons. 11. And in the fifth week of this jubilee Seth took Azura his sister to himself as wife, and in the fourth (year) she brought forth for him Enos. 12. And he began first to call upon the name of the Lord on the earth. 13. And in the seventh jubilee, in the fifth week, Enos took Noem his sister to himself as wife, and she brought forth for him a son in the third year of the fifth week, and called his name Cainan. 14. And at the end of the eighth jubilee Cainan took to himself as wife Mualet his sister, and she bore for him a son in the ninth jubilee, in the first week, in the third year of this week, and he called his name Malalel. 15. And in the second week of the tenth jubilee Malalel took unto himself as wife Sina, the daughter of Barakhel, the daughter of the sister of his father, and she bore him a son in the third week, in the sixth year, and he called his name Jared; for in his days the angels of the Lord descended upon the earth, those that are called Watchmen,* that they should teach the children of men to do judgment and right over the earth. 16. And in the eleventh jubilee Jared took to himself a wife, and her name was Baraka, a daughter of Rasujel, a daughter of the sister of his father, in the fourth week of this jubilee;

* The name by which the angels of Gen. vi. I sqq. are known in apocalyptic literature. Their evil deeds and the consequences thereof form the burden of the oldest portion of the book of Enoch. All that is here related of them and of Enoch is based upon the account there given, and the whole matter is treated **in extenso** in the writer's translation of that book. Cf. especially the Introduction, p. 32 sqq., and chap. vi. and sqq. of the book itself, together with the notes.

and she bore for him a son in the fifth week, in the fourth year, of this jubilee, and he called his name Enoch. 17. He was the first one from among the children of men that are born on the earth to learn writing and knowledge and wisdom. 18. And he wrote the signs of heaven * according to the order of their months in a book, that the sons of men might know the time of the year according to their separate months. 19. He was the first to write a testimony, and he testified to the children of men concerning the generations of the earth, and explained the weeks of the jubilees, and made known to them the days of the years, and arranged the months and explained the sabbaths of the years as we made them known to him. 20. And what was and what will be he saw in a vision of the night in a dream, and as it will happen to the children of men in their generations until the day of judgment; he saw and learned every thing and wrote it as a testimony and laid the testimony on the earth over all the children of men and for their generations. 21. And in the twelfth jubilee, in the seventh week thereof, he took to himself a wife, and her name was Edna, the daughter of Daniel, the daughter of the sister of his father; and in the sixth year in this week she bore him a son, and he called his name Methusaleh. 22. And then he was with the angels of God six years of this jubilee, and they showed him all things on earth and in heaven, the rule of the sun, and he wrote down all things. 23. And he testified to the Watchmen, those that sinned with the daughters of men; for they had commenced to mix with the daughters of the earth, so that they were defiled; and Enoch testified against them all. 24. And he was removed from the midst of the children of men, and we conducted him into the garden of Eden for greatness and for honor, and behold here he was engaged in writing down the judgment and the eternal condemnation and all the wickedness of the sons of the children of men. 25. And on his account (God) brought the deluge over the whole land of Eden;** for there he was set as a sign and that he should testify over all the sons of the children of men, that he should declare all the deeds of the generations until the day of judgment. 26. And he offered a burnt offering on the west side of the sanctuary (?) which was pleasing before the Lord on the hill of the south; for there are four places to the Lord on earth: the garden of Eden and the hill of the east in it, † and this hill on which thou art to-day, the hill of Sinai, and the hill of Zion, which will be sanctified in the new creation for a

* The standard reputation of Enoch among legend-loving Jews, Christians, and Mohammedans. Cf. Enoch (Introd.) pp. 14-17. The writing here referred to is the book of Enoch.

** This is a somewhat strange statement, and the text may be corrupt. The term "land of Eden" generally is the same as simply Eden. The connection might lead to the thought that all but Eden was then destroyed, as it was no longer inhabited since Adam's expulsion. A negative particle of some sort may have dropped out.

† Naturally the locality of the first two of these sacred places cannot be ascertained; it may be that the writer himself had no accurate idea on this matter.

sanctification of the earth: through it the earth will be sanctified from all its sin and its uncleanness to the generation of eternity.* 27. And in the fourteenth jubilee Methusaleh took unto himself as his wife Edna, the daughter of Ezrael, the daughter of the sister of his father, in the third week in the first year of this week, and he begat a son and called his name Lamech. And in the fifteenth jubilee, in the third week, Lamech took to himself a wife, and her name was Bilanos, the daughter of Barakel, the daughter of the sister of his father; and in this week she bore him a son, and he called his name Noah, saying: "This one will comfort me on account of all my work and on account of the earth which the Lord has cursed." 28. And at the end of the nineteenth jubilee, in the seventh week, in the sixth year thereof, Adam died, and all of his sons buried him in the land of the creation of Adam, and he was the first to be buried in the earth, and he lacked seventy years of one thousand years; for one thousand years are like one day in the testimony of heaven,** and therefore it was written concerning the tree of knowledge: "On the day on which ye shall eat thereof ye shall die." 29. And for this reason he did not complete the years of this day; for in it he died. 30. At the end of this jubilee Cain was killed, after him, in the same year; and his house fell upon him, and he died in the midst of the house, and he was killed with his stones, for with a stone he had killed Abel, and with a stone he was killed by a judgment of righteousness. 31. On this account it is ordained in the tablets of heaven: "With the instrument with which a man kills his neighbor, he shall be killed; as he wounded him, shall thus they do to him." † 32. And in the fifty-fifth jubilee Noah took ˙to himself a wife, and her name was Emzarah, the daughter of Rakel the daughter of his sister (sic) in the first year, in the fifth week; and in the third year thereof she bore him Shem, in the fifth year thereof she born him Ham, and in the first year in the sixth week she bore him Japhet.

CHAP. V. 1. And it happened, when the sons of the children of men commenced to increase over the face of the whole earth and daughters were born to them, that the angels of the Lord saw them in one year of this jubilee, that they were beautiful to look upon; and they took unto themselves wives from all of them whomever they chose, and they bore them sons, and these were giants. ‡ 2. And injustice increased over the earth and all flesh corrupted its way, from men to animals and to beasts and to birds and to all that walks upon the earth; all corrupted their ways and their orders and began to devour each

* Referring to the hope of all writers of Hebrew apocalypses that God would establish Israel as his ruling people on Zion, and from that centre spread his blessings over all nations. This is one of the most fixed hopes of this and similar works.

** A somewhat peculiar commentary on Ps. xc. 4.

† The **lex talionis**, based partly on Lev. xxiv. 19, 20

‡ Cf. note on iv. 15.

other, and unrighteousness increased over the earth, and all the thoughts of the knowledge of all the sons of men were thus wicked all the days. 3. And the Lord looked upon the earth, and behold it was corrupt, and all flesh corrupted its order and they all did evil before his eyes, all that were on the earth. 4. And he said: "I shall destroy mankind and all flesh that has been created above the face of the earth." And Noah alone found grace before the eyes of the Lord. 5. And concerning the angels whom he had sent upon the earth, he was greatly enraged, that he would root them out of all their power; and he said to us that we should bind them in the depths of the earth; and behold they are bound in the midst of them (depths) and separate. 6. And against their children came a word from before the face of the Lord, that they should be slain with a sword and be removed from under heaven. 7. And he said: "My spirit shall not abide over men forever, for they are flesh; and let their days be one hundred and twenty years." 8. And he sent into their midst his sword that each should slay his neighbor; and they began to slay one the other until they all fell upon the sword and were destroyed from the earth. 9. And their fathers witnessed it; and after this these were bound in the depths of the earth, until the day of the great judgment for the coming of punishment unto eternity over all those who have corrupted their ways and their works before the Lord. 10. And he destroyed all their places, and there was not left a single one of them who was not judged according to all their wickedness. 11. And he made for all of his works a new and righteous nature, so that they did not sin in their entire nature unto eternity and were righteous each in his generation all the days. 12. And the judgment of all is ordained and written on the tablets of the heaven without injustice; and all who depart from the path which is ordained for them to walk in, and if they do not walk in it, then is written down a judgment for every creature and every generation; and nothing that is in heaven, or on earth, or in the light, or in the darkness, or in Sheol, or in the depth, or in the dark place (can escape); all their judgments are ordained and written and engraved concerning all. 13. He will judge the small and the great, the great according to his greatness and the small according to his smallness, and each one according to his path. 14. And he is not one who has regard for persons, nor one who receives bribes when he says that he will hold judgment over each one: if one gives him all things on earth, he will have no regard for his person and will not receive any thing from his hands, for he is the judge. 15. And of the children of Israel it has been written and ordained, if they shall turn to him in righteousness, he will remove all their guilt and pardon all their sins. 16. It is ordained and written that he will show mercy to all who turn from all their errors, once each year. 17. And concerning all those who corrupted their ways and works before the flood, he had no regard for their persons, with the exception of Noah alone; for he had regard for his person on account of the sons whom he saved from the water of the flood for his sake;* for his heart was righteous in all his ways, as had been commanded concerning it, and he had not transgressed any thing that had been ordained for him.   18. And the Lord said: "Every thing that is on the dry land and every thing that is created, from men to animals and to beasts and to birds and to whatever moves upon the earth, shall be destroyed."   19. And he commanded Noah to build an ark for himself that he might save him from the water of the flood.   20. And Noah made an ark in every thing as he had commanded him in the (twenty-seventh) jubilee, in the fifth week, in the fifth year.   21. And he entered on the sixth (year) thereof, in the second month, in the new moon of the second month: until the sixteenth thereof he entered and all that we brought to him into the ark, and the Lord locked it from without on the seventeenth, at eve.   22. And the Lord opened the seven flood-gates of heaven and the mouths of the fountains of the great deep, seven mouths in number.   23. And the flood-gates began to pour down water from heaven forty days and forty nights, and the fountains of the deep also sent up waters, until the whole world was full of water.   24. And the water increased upon the earth: fifteen ells the waters were raised over all the high mountains, and the ark was lifted above the earth and moved upon the face of the waters.   25. And the water remained standing upon the face of the earth five months, one hundred and fifty days.   26. And the ark proceeded and rested on the top of Lubar, one of the mountains of Ararat.   27. And in the fourth month the fountains of the great deep were closed, and the flood-gates of heaven were restrained, and in the new moon of the seventh month all the mouths of the deep of the earth were opened, and the water began to descend into the deep below.   28. And in the new moon of the tenth month the tops of the mountains became visible, and in the new moon of the first month the earth became visible.   29. And the waters disappeared from above the earth in the fifth week, in the seventh year thereof, and on the seventeenth day in the second month the earth became dry.   30. And on the twenty-seventh thereof he opened the ark and sent out of it the animals and the beasts and the birds and whatever moves.

CHAP. VI.   1. And at the new moon of the third month he came out of the ark and built an altar on that hill.   2. And he appeared on the earth, and he took a young goat and atoned by its blood for all the guilt of the earth, because every thing that had been on it was destroyed except those that were in the ark with Noah; and he placed the fat on the altar, and he took an ox and a goat and a sheep and young goats and salt and a turtle dove and the young of a dove and brought a burnt sacrifice upon the altar and scattered over them fruit offerings

* I. e., Noah's sons were not themselves worthy of being saved, but escaped death for their father's sake.

baked in oil and sprinkled the blood and wine, and placed upon it frankincense, and a sweet savour arose which was acceptable before the Lord. 3. And the Lord smelt the sweet savour, and he made with him a covenant that there should no more be a flood upon the earth which would destroy the earth: all the days of the earth, seed and harvest shall not cease, frost and heat and summer and winter and day and night shall not change their order and shall not cease forever. 4. "And ye, grow and increase on the earth and increase over it, and be for a blessing in its midst: your fear and your terror I will put upon every thing that is on the earth and in the sea. 5. And, behold, I have given you all the animals and all the beasts and every thing that flies and every thing that moves on the earth and the fish in the waters and all things for food; like the herbs of grass, I have given them all to you to eat. 6. Only flesh which is in its life with blood ye shall not eat: for the blood is the soul of all flesh, so that your blood in your souls be not demanded of you. 7. From the hands of each one I will demand the blood of a man; every one that sheddeth the blood of a man, by the hand of a man shall his blood be shed; for in the image of God did he create Adam. 8. But ye, grow and increase upon the earth." 9. And Noah and his sons swore that they would not eat any blood that is in any flesh, and they made a covenant before the Lord God for ever, in all the generations of the world, in this month. 10. On this account he spoke to thee that thou shouldst make a covenant with the children of Israel in this month upon the mountain, with an oath, and shouldst sprinkle blood over them on account of all the words of the covenant which the Lord has made with them for all days.* 11. And this testimony is written concerning you, that you observe it in all days, that ye do not in all days eat any blood of animals and birds and beasts in all the days of the earth; and the man who eats the blood of an animal or of beasts or of birds in all the days of the earth, he and his seed shall be rooted out of the land. 12. And thou command the children of Israel that they shall not eat any blood, so that their names and their seed may be before the Lord our God all the days. 13. And for this law there is no limit of days, for it is for eternity; and they shall observe it to generation and generation, so that they may continue supplicating in their behalf with blood before the Lord on the altar on each day and day; mornings and evenings they shall supplicate in their behalf perpetually before the Lord, that they may observe this and not be rooted out. 14. And he gave to Noah and his sons a sign that there should not again be a deluge over the earth; he placed his bow in the clouds as a sign of the eternal covenant that no water of the deluge should again come over the earth to destroy it all the days of the earth. 15. On this account it is ordained and written on the tablets of heaven that the celebration of the festival of weeks should be in this month, once a year, for a renewed covenant in each year and

* The covenant of Sinai is regarded as a renewal of the Noachic covenant.

year.*   16. And during the time this festival was being celebrated in heaven, from the days of creation to the days of Noah, it was twenty-six jubilees and five weeks of years; and Noah and his sons observed it seven jubilees and one week of years until the time when Noah died. 17. But his children violated it until the days of Abraham, and they ate blood. But Abraham alone observed it, and Isaac and Jacob observed it, for these are his children, up to thy day; and in thy day the children of Israel forgot it until I renewed it for them on this mountain. 18. And thou command the children of Israel that they should observe this festival in all their generations as a commandment for them: one day in the year, in this month, they shall celebrate this festival. 19. For it is the festival of weeks and is a festival of first fruits; for this festival is of a double nature and double kind, as is written and engraved concerning its celebration.   20. For I have written it in the book of the first law in which I write to thee that thou shouldst observe it in its time one day a year; and I have explained to thee the offerings on that day, that they should be remembered and that the children of Israel should celebrate it one day in each year.   21. And at the new moon of the first month, and in the new moon of the fourth month, and in the new moon of the seventh month, and in the new moon of the tenth month are the days of remembrance and the days of the festivals in the four divisions of the years: written and ordained they are for a testimony until eternity.   22. And Noah ordained them for himself as festivals for future generations, for on them there was to him a remembrance.   23. At the new moon of the first month it was said to him that he should make for himself an ark, and on it the earth became dry, and he opened (the ark) and saw the earth. And at the new moon of the fourth month the mouth of the flood-gates of the earth were opened and the waters began to descend into the depth beneath. 25. And at the new moon of the tenth month the tops of the mountains appeared, and Noah became glad.   26. And on this account he ordained them as festivals of remembrance unto himself unto eternity, and thus they are ordained.   27. And they were raised into the tablets of heaven: thirteen sabbaths to each, from one to another their remembrance, from the first to the second, from the second to the third, from the third to the fourth.   28. And all the days of this commandment are fifty-two sabbaths of days, and the whole year is completed.   29. Thus it is engraved and ordained in the tablets of heaven, and there is no transgression from one year to another. And thou command the children of Isral that they should observe the years in this number, three hundred and sixty-four days, and the year shall be complete and the fixed date of their days and their festivals shall not be corrupted, for every thing transpires in them according to their testimony, and they (Israel) shall not miss a day or corrupt a festival.

* It will be observed here and throughout the book that the author connects the religious system and worship in Israel not only with the ordinances of the tablets of heaven, but also with important events in the lives of the patriarchs.

31. But if they do transgress and do not observe them according to his commandment, then will be corrupted all their fixed dates, and the years will waver in consequence, and also their times and their years, and they will transgress their ordinances. 32. And all the children of Israel will forget and will not find the paths of the years, and will forget the new moon and the sabbaths and the festivals, and in all the order of the years they will err. 33. For I know, and from now on I shall make it known to thee, and not from my heart, but thus is written in a book before me and is ordained in the tablets of heaven, the division of days, that they forget not the festivals of my covenant and walk according to the festivals of the Gentiles, after their errors and after their ignorance. 34. And there will be those who will make observations of the moon, for this one (the moon) corrupts the stated times and comes out earlier each year by ten days. 35. And in this way they will corrupt the years and will observe a wrong day as the day of testimony and a corrupted festival day, and every one will mix holy days with unclean ones and unclean with holy; for they will err as to months and sabbaths and festivals and jubilees. 36. And on this account I command thee and testify to thee that thou shouldst testify to them, for after thy death thy children will corrupt, so that they make a year only three hundred and sixty-four days,* and on this account they will err as to new moons and sabbaths and fixed times and festivals and will ever eat blood with all kinds of flesh.

CHAP. VII. 1. And in the seventh week, in the first year thereof, in this jubilee, Noah planted vines on this hill upon which the ark had rested, named Lubar, the Ararat Mountains, and they produced fruit in the fourth year, and he watched their fruit and gathered them in this year in the seventh month, and he made wine of it, and put it into a vessel and kept it until the fifth year, until the first day of the new moon of the first month. 2. And he celebrated this day in rejoicing as a festival,**and he made a sacrifice unto the Lord, a young one from among the oxen and a ram and a sheep, each seven years old, and a young goat, that he might thereby obtain pardon for himself and his sons. 3. And he prepared the goat first, and he placed of its blood upon the flesh of the altar which he had made, and all the fat he laid upon the altar where he was sacrificing to the Lord, and of the ox and the sheep he also placed the flesh upon the altar. 4. And he made all the fruit offerings thereof mixed with oil upon them, and thereupon he first scattered wine upon the fire on the altar, and placed incense upon the altar, and a sweet savour ascended which was acceptable before the Lord his God. 5. And he and his children rejoiced and drank of this wine in joy. † 6. And it was evening, and he went into

* How this statement is to be reconciled with verse 30 is not clear.

** Cf. chap. vi. vs. 21 and 22.

† The writer apologetically describes the wine as having been drunk by Noah on the occasion of a religious festival.

his tent, and he lay down drunken, and he slept, and he was uncovered in his tent while sleeping. 7. And Ham saw his father naked, and going out he told it to his two brothers without. 8. And Shem took his garment and arose, he and Japheth, and they carried the garment upon their shoulders, and their faces backward, and covered the shame of their father. 9. And Noah awoke from his sleep and learned everything that his youngest sons had done to him; and he cursed his son and said: "Cursed be Canaan, a slaving servant shall he be to his brothers." And he blessed Shem: "Blessed be the Lord God of Shem, and may Canaan be his servant; and may the Lord extend Japheth and may the Lord dwell in the tent of Shem, and Canaan shall be his servant!" 11. And Ham knew that his father had cursed his youngest son, and he became displeased with him because he had cursed his son and he separated himself from his father, he and his sons with him, Chush, and Meshrem, and Pud, and Canaan. 12. And he built for himself a city, and called its name after the name of his wife Neelata-Mek.* 13. And Japheth saw it and became envious of his brother, and he too built a city, and called its name after the name of his wife Adalenses. 14. But Shem dwelt with his father Noah, and he built a city by the side of his father on the hill, and he too called its name by the name of his wife Sedukatelbab. 15. And behold these three cities are near Mount Lubar: Sedukatelbab on the side of the hill on the east; Neultemauk on the south side; and Adalaneses toward the west; and these are the sons of Shem: Elam, and Asur, and Arpakeed: this is the generation after the second year of the flood(?)** . . . these are the children of Noah. 16. And in the twenty-eighth jubilee he began to command the sons of his sons the ordinances and the commandments all as he had learned them and the judgments, and he testified to his sons that they should observe righteousness, and that they should cover the shame of their flesh, and that they should bless him who created them, and should honor father and mother, and each should love his neighbor, and should preserve their souls from all fornication and from all uncleanness and unrighteousness. 17. For on account of these three things the deluge came over the earth, namely on account of fornication, in which the Watchmen indulged against the commandments of their law, with the daughters of men, and took to themselves wives from all whom they chose and made the beginning of uncleanness. 18. And they began sons, the Naphidem, and they were all unlike and they devoured one another: the giant slew the Naphil, and the Naphil slew Eljo, and Eljo the children of men, and all publicly practised every unrighteousness and shed much blood, and the earth was filled with unrighteousness; and after

* Very little reliance can be placed upon these names as the MSS. vary, and nearly all trace of the etymology is lost. The copyists naturally made mistakes in writing them.

** Here is a **lacuna** in the Ethiopic text.

all these the animals, and the beasts, and the birds, and whatever walks and moves on the earth; and much blood was spilt on the earth, and all the thoughts and deeds of men were wicked in all the days. 19. And the Lord destroyed everything from the face of the earth on account of their deeds and on account of the blood which was spilt over the earth. 20. And we were left, I and you, my sons, and everything that entered with us into the ark, and behold I am the first to see your works that ye do not walk in righteousness, for in the path of destruction have you commenced to walk, and are separating yourselves each from his neighbor, and are envious the one of the other, and are not in harmony each with his neighbor and his brother. 21. And yet, my sons, for I see and behold the satans have commenced to lead astray you and your children; and now I fear on your behalf that after my death ye will spill the blood of men over the face of the earth, and that ye too will be destroyed from its face. 22. For every one that sheds the blood of any man, and every one that eats the blood in any flesh, shall all be destroyed from the earth. 23. And there shall not be left any man who eats blood and who sheds blood upon the earth, and there shall not be left alone for him any seed or children under heaven; for they will go into Sheol, and into the place of judgment they will descend, in the darkness of the deep they will all be cast by a terrible death. 24. With regard to all blood over you which is in all the days that ye sacrifice an animal or a beast or whatever flies over the earth, and do a good deed concerning your souls in your covering of that which has been spilt over the face of the earth. 25. And ye shall not be like him that eats with blood; be strong that no one eat blood in your presence: bury the blood in the earth; for as I have been commanded, I testify to you and your children together with all flesh. 26. And ye shall not eat the soul with the meat, that ye be not those of whom your blood, that is, your soul, be demanded from the hands of every one that sheddeth blood on the earth. 27. For the earth will not be clean of the blood which has been spilt upon it, but only by the blood of him that shed it will the earth be cleansed in all the generations of the earth. 28. And now, my children, obey and practise righteousness and justice so that ye be planted in righteousness upon the whole face of the earth, and that your renown be elevated before my God who has saved me from the water of the deluge. 29. And, behold, ye will proceed and build for yourselves cities and will plant in them all that bears fruit; for three years its fruit shall not be gathered to eat it, and in the fourth year the fruit shall be sanctified, and the first fruits which they gather shall be brought before the Lord our God, the Most High, who created heaven and earth and all things, so that they bring in fatness the first of the wine and oil as first fruits upon the altar of the Lord who receives it; and what is left the servants of the house of the Lord shall eat before the altar which he has accepted. 30. And in the fifth year make the release, so that ye release them in righteousness and justice, and you shall be just and all your plants shall be right. 31. For thus did Enoch the father of your father Methusaleh, command his sons, and Methusaleh his son Lamech, and Lamech commanded me all the things which his father commanded him; but I command it to you, my children, just as Enoch commanded his son in his first jubilee; while he was alive, in his generation the seventh, he commanded and testified to his son and to the sons of his sons until the day of his death.

CHAP. VIII. 1. In the twenty-ninth jubilee, in the first week, in the first (year) thereof, Arphaksed took to himself a wife, and her name was Rasuja, the daughter of Susan, the daughter of Elam, and she bore him a son in the third year of this week, and he called his name Kainan. 2. And his son grew, and his father taught him writing, and he went to seek for himself a place where he might seize for himself a city. 3. And he found a writing which the forefathers had carved into a rock, and he read what was in it, and he translated it and found that there was within it the science of the Watchmen by which they had seen the astrology of the sun and the moon and the stars and in all the signs of heaven;* and he wrote this down and did not say any thing concerning it, for he feared to speak to Noah con cerning it, lest he be angry with him on this account. 4. And in the thirtieth jubilee, in the second week, in the first year thereof, he took to himself a wife, and her name was Milka, the daughter of Abadai, the son of Japhet, and in the fourth year she bore him a son, and he called his name Sala, for he said, "Verily, I have been sent away." 5. And in the fourth year Sala was born, and he grew up and took to himself a wife, and her name was Muak, the daughter of Kesed, the brother of his father, in the thirty-first jubilee, in the first week, in the first year thereof. And she bore him a son in the fifth year, and he called his name Ebor; and he took to himself a wife, and her name was Azurad, the daughter of Nebrod, in the thirty-second jubilee, in the seventh week, in the third year thereof. 6. And in the sixth year thereof she bore him a son, and he called his name Phalek, for in the days when he was born the children of Noah began to divide the earth among themselves; and on this account he called his name Phalek. 7. And they divided the earth among themselves in wickedness, and told it to Noah. 8. And it happened in the beginning of the thirty-third jubilee, and they divided the earth into three parts, to Shem and to Ham, and to Japhet, each one his inheritance, in the first year of the first week, while an angel, one of us who were sent to them, was there. 9. And he called his sons, and they came to him, they and their children, and he divided the earth by lot what his three sons should take, and they stretched out their hands and took to themselves the writing out of the bosom of their father Noah. 10. And there came

* Cf. Book of Enoch, c. viii. 1 sqq.

out on the writing as the lot for Shem the middle of the earth, which he and his children should have as an inheritance for the generations unto eternity, from the middle of the Mountain Rafu, from the exit of the water of the river Tina, and his portion goes toward the west through the midst of this river, and they go until they approach to the abyss of the waters out of which comes this river, and this river empties and pours its waters into the sea Miot, and this river goes into the great sea: all that is toward the north of this is Japhet's, and all that is to the direction of the south is Shem's.   11. And it reaches until it comes to Karaso, which is in the bosom of the tongue which looks toward the south.   12. And his portion reaches unto the great sea, and reaches straight until it approaches the west of the tongue which looks toward the south; for the sea is called the tongue of the Egyptian sea.   13. And it turns from there toward the south, toward the mouth of the great sea in the shore of the waters and proceeds toward Arabia and Ophra, and it proceeds until it reaches to the water of the river Gejon and toward the south of the water of Gejon, along the shore of this same river.   14. And it proceeds toward the north until it approaches the garden of Eden, toward the south thereof to the south, and from the east of the whole land of Eden, and toward the whole east, and it turns to the east, and proceeds until it approaches toward the east of the hills whose name is Rafa, and it descends toward the border of the outlet of the water of the river Tina.   15. This portion came out in the lot for Shem and his sons, and he remembered his word which he had spoken with his mouth in prophecy, for he had said: "Blessed be the Lord God of Shem, and may the Lord dwell in the dwelling of Shem!"   17. And he knew that the garden of Eden is the holy of holies, and the dwelling of the Lord, and Mount Sinai, the centre of the desert, and Mount Zion, the centre of the navel of the earth,* these three, opposite one another, were created as sanctuaries. 18. And he blessed the God of gods who had put the speech of the Lord into his mouth.   19. And he knew that a blessed portion and a blessing had come to Shem and to the children of his generations forever; the whole land of Edom, and all the land of the Erythrian sea, and all the land of the east, and India and at the Erythrian and the mountains thereof, and all the land of Basor, and all the land of Lebanon and the islands of Kuphatur, and all the land of Elam and Asur and Babel and Susan and Madar, and all the mountains of Ararat, and all the land beyond the sea which is beyond the hills of Asur toward the north, a blessed and prosperous land, and all that is in it is very good.   20. And for Ham came out as the second portion, beyond the Gijon, toward the south, to the right of the garden, and it proceeds to all the fire mountains, and goes toward the west to the

* That Jerusalem is the centre of the earth is an idea often met with in the later Jewish writers, and it is therefore also the central place of the Messianic rule. Cf., e. g., Enoch, lvi. 7; Dillmann, Aethiop. Chrest., p. 15.

sea Atil, and goes to the west until it reaches to the sea of Mauk, of that one into which everything descends that is destroyed. 21. And it proceeds to the north to the shore of Gadil and goes to the west of the water of the sea until it approaches the river Gejon, and the river Gejon goes until it approaches to the right of the garden of Eden: and this land is the land which came forth for Ham as the portion he shall retain for himself and the children of his generations forever. 22. And for Japhet there came forth a third portion beyond the river Tina, toward the north of the exit of its waters, and it goes toward the northeast the whole district of Lag, and all the east thereof. 23. And it goes toward the north to the north, and goes to the mountains of Kilt, toward the north and toward the sea Mauk, and it goes toward the east of Gadir over toward the coast of the water of the sea. 24. And it proceeds until it approaches the west of Para, and returns toward Apherag, and goes toward the east, towards the waters of the sea Meat. And it goes toward the shore of the river Tina, toward the east of the north, until it approaches to the shore of the waters thereof, toward the mountain Rafa, and it bends toward the north. 25. This is the land which came forth for Japhet and his children as the portion of his inheritance which he should hold unto eternity for himself and the children of their generation unto eternity: five great islands and a great land in the north; only it is cold, but the land of Ham is hot, and the land of Shem has neither heat nor frost, for it is mixed in coldness and heat.

CHAP. IX. 1. And Ham divided among his sons; and the first portion came out for Ques toward the east, and to the west of him for Phud, and to the west of him for Kainan toward the west of the sea. 2. And Shem also divided among his sons, and the first portion came forth for Elam and his sons toward the east of the river Tiger, until it approaches the east, the whole land of India and on the Erythrian and its coast, and the waters of Dedan and all the mountains of Mebri and Ela, and all the land of Susan, and all that is on the side of the Phernak to the Erythrian sea and the river Tina. 3. But for Asur came forth a second portion, all the land of Asur and Nineva and Sinaor and to the border of India, and ascends along the river. 4. And for Arphaksed came forth a third portion, all the land of the district of the Chaldees toward the east of the Euphrates, bordering on the Erythrian sea, and all the waters of the desert until near to the tongue of the sea which looks toward Egypt, and all the sand of Lebanon and Saner and Amana to the border of the Euphrates. 5. And for Aram came forth as a fourth portion all the land of Mesopotamia, between the Tiger and the Euphrates, toward the north of the Chaldees, to the border of the mountains of Asur. 6. And the land of Arara came out as a fifth portion to his son, the mountains of Asur and all belonging to them until it reaches to the east of Asur, his brother. 7. And Japhet, too, divided the land of his inheritance between his sons, and the first portion came forth for Gomer toward the east, from the north side to the river Tina. And in the north there came out for Magog all the inner portions of the north until it reaches the sea Meat.   8. And for Madai came forth as his portion that he should possess, to the west of his two brothers, unto the islands and unto the coasts of the islands. And to Egawan came forth as a fourth portion all the islands, and the islands which are toward Edalud.   9. And for Tobel came forth as a fifth portion, between the tongue which approaches toward the side of the portion of Lud, to the second tongue, unto beyond the second tongue into the third tongue.   10. And for Melek came forth as a sixth portion, all that beyond the third tongue, until it approaches to the east of Gadir.   11. And for Tiras came forth a seventh portion; four great islands in the midst of the sea, which approach to the portion of Ham; and the islands of Kamatura came out for the sons of Arphaksed in his division of his inheritance by lot.   12. And thus the sons of Noah divided out to their children, in the presence of Noah their father, and he caused them to swear an oath cursing him who endeavored to seize a portion which had not been alloted him. And they all said: "Thus be it! Thus be it!" for themselves and for their descendants to eternity in their generations, until the day of judgment, on which the Lord God will judge them with a sword and with fire for all the wickedness of uncleanness which they have committed in that they filled the earth with transgression, uncleanness, fornication, and sin.

CHAP. X.   1. And in the third week of this jubilee the evil demons began to lead astray the sons of Noah and deceived them and destroyed them.   2. And the sons came to Noah their father and told him concerning the demons which were leading astray, darkening, and slaying the sons of their sons.   3. And he prayed before the Lord his God, and he said: "Lord of the spirits* of all flesh, thou who hast shown mercy to me and hast delivered me and my children from the waters of the deluge, and hast not suffered me to be destroyed as thou didst the children of destruction, for thy grace was great over men, and great was thy mercy over my soul; may thy grace be exalted over the sons of thy sons, and may the evil spirit not rule over them to destroy them off the earth. And thou hast verily blessed me and my sons that we increase and multiply and fill the earth.   4. And thou knowest how the Watchmen, the fathers of these spirits, acted in my day; and these spirits also which are alive, cast them into prison and hold them in the places of judgment, and let them not destroy the sons of thy servant, my God, for they are terrible and created for destroying; and may they not rule over the spirits of the living; for thou alone knowest their judgment.   5. And let them have no sway over the children of the righteous from now on and to eternity.   6. And our God said unto us that we should bind all.   7. And the angel

* A typical name of God in the Parables of Enoch, c. xxxvii. 71.

of the spirits, Mastema,* came and said: "O Lord, Creator, leave some of them before me, and they shall hear my voice and they shall do all things that I tell them; for if thou dost not leave any of them to me I shall not be able to accomplish the power of my will among the children of men, for they are here for corrupting, and destroying, and leading astray before the judgment, for great is their wickedness to the children of men." 8. And he said: "The tenth part of them shall be left before him and nine parts shall descend into the place of judgment." 9. And one of us said: "We will teach Noah all their medicines;" for they did not walk in righteousness, and did not contend in uprightness. And we did according to his word; all the wicked ones that were terrible we bound in the place of judgment, but the tenth part of them we left, that they should be judged before Satan on the earth. 10. And the medicines of all their sicknesses we explained to Noah together with all their deceptions how to heal them with the plants of the earth. 11. And Noah wrote all these down in a book as we instructed him, concerning every kind of medicines, and the evil spirits were held away from the sons of Noah. 12. And he gave all the writings which he had written to Shem, his oldest son, for him he loved exceedingly above all his children. 13. And Noah slept with his fathers and was buried on Mount Lubar, in the land of Ararat. 14. Nine hundred and fifty years he completed in his life; nineteen jubilees and two weeks and five years; he excelled in his life on the earth the children of men on account of his righteousness, in which he was perfect, with the exception of Enoch. 15. For the history of Enoch is made a testimony to the generations of eternity to announce all the deeds of the generation on the day of judgment. 16. In the thirty-third (fourth) jubilee, in the first year of the second week, Phalek took to himself a wife, whose name was Lamna, the daughter of Sinaar, and she bore him a son in the fourth year of this week, and he called his name Ragev, for he said: "Behold, the sons of men have become evil through a plan of wickedness, because they build for themselves a city and a tower in the land of Sinaar;" for they separated from the land of Ararat toward the east to Sinaar, for in his day they were building a city and a tower, saying: "We will ascend on it into heaven." 17. And they began to build in the fourth week, and they burned with fire, and they used bricks for stones, and the clay with which they joined them was asphalt, which comes out of the sea and out of the fountains of water in the land of Sinaar, and they built forty years, and three years they were making bricks. . . 18. And the Lord our God said to us: "Behold it is one people that has commenced

* The name of the leader of the evil spirits found throughout the book. The role here occupied by him may have been taken from that of Satan in Job, but it is in place to remark that in many apocryphal works, especially in Enoch, demonology has a wide field and the satans are recognized as organized opponents of God, who, however, do their evil deeds only with his permission. The word Mastema is derived from שטם ═ שטן, the Greek form being μαστιφάτ.

to do it, and now I shall not let go of them; behold, we will descend and mix their tongues, and one shall not hear the other and they shall be scattered into cities and into nations and one counsel shall no longer abide with them until the day of judgment." 19. And the Lord descended, and we descended with him to see the city and tower which the children of men were building. 20. And he confounded all the speech of their tongues, and they no longer heard the voice one of the other, and they ceased then to build the city and the tower. On this account the whole land of Sinaar is called Babel, because there God confused all the tongues of the children of men, and from there they were scattered to all their cities, each according to his language and his nation. And the Lord sent a great wind against the tower and it overturned it upon the ground, and behold, (it stood) between the land of Assur and Babylon in the land of Sinaar, and they called its name Ruins. 21. And in the fourth week, in the first year of the thirty-fourth jubilee they were scattered out of the land of Sinaar. 22. And Ham and his sons went into the land which he had taken, which fell to him by lot in the land of the north (south); and Kainaan saw the land of the Libanon to the canal of Egypt that it was very good, and he did not go into the land of his inheritance to the west of the sea, and dwelt in the land of Libanon on the coast of the sea. 23. And Ham, his father, and Cush and Mezrem, his brothers, said to him: "Thou hast settled in a land which is not thine and did not fall to us by lot, thou shouldst not do thus; for if thou doest thus, then thou and thy children will fall by condemnation in the land, and as cursed ones by sedition, for by sedition ye have settled and by sedition thy children will fall and thou wilt be rooted out to eterntiy. 24. Do not dwell in the dwelling place of Shem, for to Shem and his children was it given by lot. 25. Cursed art thou and cursed shalt thou be above all the sons of Noah by the curse which we covenanted with an oath between us in the presence of the holy judge and before Noah our father." 26. But he did not listen to them and dwelt in the land of Libanon from Emath to the entrance of Egypt, he and his sons until this day. 27. And on this account this land is called Canaan. 28. But Japheth and his sons went toward the east and dwelt in their portions and Madi saw the land of the sea, and it pleased him, and he begged it from Elam, and Assur, and Arphaksed, the brother of his wife, and he dwelt in the land Medkin, near to the brother of his wife until this day. 29. And he called his dwelling place and the dwelling place of his sons Madakia, by the name of their father Madai.

CHAP. XI. 1. In the thirty-fifth jubilee, in the third week, in the first year thereof, Ragev took unto himself a wife, and her name was Ora, the daughter of Or, the daughter of the son of Kesed, and she bore him a son, and he called his name Serug, in the seventh year of this week of this jubilee. 2. And the sons of Noah began to fight with each other, to take captive and to slay each one his brother, and to spill the blood of men over the earth, and to eat blood, and to build strong cities, and walls, and towers (and single men elevated themselves above the people, and first founded kingdoms), and to make war, a nation against a nation, and nations against nations, and city against city, and all things became worse, and they acquired for themselves arms, and taught their sons war, and began to take captive the cities and to sell male and female slaves.   3. And Ur, the son of Kesed, built Era of the Chaldees, and called its name after his own name and by the name of his father.   4. And he made for himself molten images, and they worshipped each one his own image which they had made for themselves by molding, and they began to make sculptured images and unclean forms, and the terrible spirits assisted them and misled them to commit transgression and uncleanness. 5. And the prince Mastema gave his power to make all this, and through the angels who had been given under his hand, he sent out his hand to do all wickedness and sin and all transgression, and to destroy and to murder and to shed blood over the earth.   6. On this account his name was called Serach, for Serach turned himself in all things to do all kinds of sin.   7. And he grew and dwelt in Ur of the Chaldees near to the father of the mother of his wife, and he worshipped idols, and he took to himself a wife in the thirty-sixth jubilee, in the fifth week, in the first year thereof, and her name was Melka, the daughter of Keher, the daughter of the brother of his father. And she bore him a son Nakor, in the first year of this week, and he grew and dwelt in Ur of the Chaldees, and his father taught him the researches of the Chaldees, divination and astrology according to the signs of the heavens.   8. And in the thirty-seventh jubilee, in the sixth week, in the first year thereof, he took to himself a wife, and her name was Ijosek, the daughter of Nesteg of the Chaldees.   9. And she bore him Tarah in the seventh year of this week.   10. And the prince Mastema sent ravens and birds that they should eat what was sown on the land, in order to destroy the land, so that they might deprive the children of men of their labor, for before they plowed in the seed the ravens picked it up from the surface of the ground. 11. On that account his father called his name Tarah, because the ravens and the birds robbed them and devoured their seed.   12. And the years began to be barren on account of the birds, and all the fruit of the trees they ate from the trees; with great strength they were able to save a little from all the fruit of the land in their days.   13. And in the thirty-ninth jubilee, in the second week, in the first year, Tarah took to himself a wife, and her name was Edna, the daughter of Abram, the daughter of the sister of his father.   14. And in the seventh year of this week she bore him a son, and he called his name Abram by the name of the father of his mother, for he had died before his daughter conceived a son.   15. And the child began to understand the errors of the earth, that all went astray after the images and after uncleanness; and his father taught him writing when two weeks of years old; and he separated himself from his father that he might not worship the idols with him.   16. And he began to pray to the Creator of all things that he should save him from the errors of the children of men, and that his portion should not fall into error after uncleanness and shame.   17. And the time of seed came to sow it upon the land, and all came out together to watch their seed against the ravens, and Abram came out with those that came out, and he was a boy of fourteen years.   18. And a cloud of ravens came to devour the seed, and Abram ran to scatter them before they sat down on the earth to eat the seed, and said: "Do not devour; return to the place whence you came!" and they turned back.   19. And clouds of ravens returned that day seven times, and of all the ravens none sat down upon any of the land where Abram was, and not one was left there.   20. And all those that were with him on the whole land saw him crying, and all the ravens turned back, and great was his name in all the land of the Chaldees.   21. And there came to him in this year all those that had sowed seed, and he would go with them until the time sowing in the land ceased, and they sowed in their land, and in this year they brought home grain, and ate it and were satisfied.   22. And in the fifth year of the fifth week Abram taught those who make the instruments for oxen, the workmen in wood, and they made utensils over the earth, opposite the crook timber of the plows in order to put the seed thereon, and to let the seed fall out of it into the seed furrows. 23. And it was hidden in the earth, and they no longer feared the ravens; and thus they did on all the crook-timber of the plows over the earth, and they sowed and worked the land each one as Abram had commanded them, and no longer feared the ravens.

CHAP. XII.   1. And it happened in the sixth week, in the seventh year thereof, Abram said unto Tarah, his father, saying, "Father!" And he said, "Behold, here I am, my son!"   2. And he said: "What assistance and what pleasure have we from all the idols which thou dost worship and before which thou dost prostrate thyself?   3. For there is no spirit in them, but they are dumb statues and a deception of the heart: do not worship them.   4. Worship the God of heaven, who sends down dew and rain upon the earth and does everything upon the earth and has created everything through his word and all living things are from before his face.   5. Why do ye worship those who have no heart and spirit in them; for they are the works of hands, and upon your shoulders do ye carry them, and ye have from them no help, but a great disgrace to those who make them and a deception of the heart to those who worship them: do not worship them!" 6. And Tarah said: "I also know it, my son; but what shall I do with this people who command me that I should serve them?   7. If I tell them the truth, they will slay me; for their soul clings to them to worship and to glorify them.   8. Keep silent, my son, lest they slay thee!" 9. And these words he spoke to his two brothers, and they became angry at him, and he kept silent. 10. And in the fortieth jubilee, in the second week, in the seventh year thereof, Abram took to himself a wife, and her name was Sara, the daughter of his father, and she became to him a wife. 11. And Aran, his brother, took to himself (a wife) in the third year of this week, and his wife bare him a son in the seventh year of this week, and he called his name Lot. 12. And Nachor also, his brother, took to himself a wife. 13. And in the (sixtieth) year of the life of Abram, that is, in the fourth year of the fourth week, Abram arose in the night, and burned down the house of his idols, and burned all that was in the house, and there was no man that knew it. 14. And they arose in the night and desired to' save their idols from the midst of the flame. 15. And Aran ran in order to save them, and the fire burned over him and he burned in the midst of the fire, and he died in Ur of the Chaldees before Tarah, his father, and they buried him in Ur. 16. And Tarah went away from Ur of the Chaldees, he and his sons, in order to come into the land of the Lebanon and into the land of Canaan; and he dwelt in Haran, and Abram dwelt with his father Tarah in Haran two weeks of years. 17. And in the sixth week, in the fifth year thereof, Abram arose and sat in the night at the new moon of the seventh month, so that he might observe the stars from the evening to the morning, so that he might know what would be the character of the year with regard to the rains, and he was sitting alone and observing. 18. And a word came into his heart, and he said: "All the signs of the stars and the signs of the sun and of the moon are all in the hand of the Lord; why do I search them out? 19. If he desires, he causes it to rain, morning and evening; and if he desires, he causes it to descend, and all things are in his hands." 20. And he prayed in that night, and said: "My God, God Most High, thou alone art a God to me, and thou hast created all things, and all things that are are the works of thy hand, and thee and thy godship have I chosen. 21. Deliver me from the hands of the evil spirits who reign over the thoughts of the hearts of men, and let them not lead me astray from thee, my God, and cause thou me and my seed in eternity not to go astray from now on and to eternity! 22. And I say, shall I return to Ur of the Chaldees, who seek my face, that I should return to them; or shall I remain here in this place; the right path before thee prosper in the hands of thy servant, that he may follow it and now walk in the error of my heart, O my God!" 23. He completed his words and prayer, and, behold, the Lord sent a word to him through me, saying: Up, go thou out of thy country, and out of thy kindred, and out of the house of thy father, into a land which I will show to thee, and I will make thee in the land which is great into a great and numerous people. 24. And I will bless thee and will make thy name great, and thou shalt be blessed in the land, and all the nations of the earth shall be blessed in thee; those that bless thee I will bless, and those that curse thee I will curse.

25. And I will be a God to thee and to thy children and to thy children's children and to all thy seed, and behind thee will be thy God. 26. Fear not, from now on to all the generations of the earth I am thy God." 27. And the Lord God said to me: "Open his mouth and his ears that he may hear and speak with the language which has been revealed;" for it had ceased from the mouths of all the children of men. 28. And I opened his mouth and his lips, and I opened his ears, and I began to speak with him in Hebrew, in the tongue of creation; and he took the books of his father, and these were written in Hebrew, and he copied them, and he began to learn them from then on, and I made known to him every thing he was incapable (of understanding), and he studied them the six months of the rainy period. 29. And it happened in the seventh year of the sixth week, and he spoke with his father, and informed him that he would go from Haran to go to the land of Canaan to see it and to return to him. 30. And Tarah, his father, said to him: "Go in peace! the God of the worlds make straight thy path, and the Lord be with thee and protect thee from all evil, and give to thee good will and mercy and grace before those who see thee; and may none of the sons of men come over thee to do thee evil; go in peace! 31. And if thou seest a land pleasant to thy eyes to dwell in it, then up, and take me with thee; and take Lot with thee, the son of Aran thy brother, as thy son, and God be with thee. 32. But Nachor thy brother leave with me until thou returnest in peace and we go with thee together."

CHAP. XIII. 1. And Abram went from Haran, and took Sara, his wife, and Lot, the son of his brother Aran, to the land of Canaan, and he came into the land of Asur, and proceeded to Sakimon, and dwelt near a great oak. And he saw the land, and, behold, it was very beautiful from the entrance of Emet to the great mountains. 2. And the Lord said to him: "To thee and to thy seed I will give this land." 3. And he built an altar there, and brought upon it a sacrifice to the Lord who had appeared to him. 4. And he arose from there, with the hill Bethel toward the sea (west), and Ai to the east, and fixed his tent there. 5. And he saw, and, behold, the land was pleasant and extended and very wide, and every thing grew on it, vines and figs and pomegranates and terebinths and oil trees and cedars and Lebanon trees and cypresses and all the trees of the field; and water was upon the hills. 6. And he blessed the Lord who had led him out of Ur of the Chaldees and brought him to this hill. 7. And it happened in the first year, in the seventh week, at the new moon of the first month, that he built an altar on this hill, and called upon the name of the Lord: "Thou art my God, the God unto eternity." 8. And he placed upon the altar a sacrifice unto the Lord, that he should be with him and should not desert him all the days of his life. 9. And he arose from there and went toward the north,* and he came to Hebron,

* It should be "southward," — probably a blunder of a translator living in Ethiopia.

and Hebron was built at that time,* and he dwelt there two years in the land to the north of Boa-Lot, and there was a famine in the land, and Abram went into Egypt in the third year of this week, and he dwelt in Egypt five years before his wife was torn away from him. 10. But Tani* *\|in Egypt was\|then built in the seventh winter after Hebron. 11. And it happened that when Pharoah seized Sara, the wife of Abram, the Lord punished Pharoah and his whole house with large plagues, on account of Sara, the wife of Abram. And Abram was very conspicuous by wealth in sheep and oxen and asses and horses and camels and in man-servants and in maid-servants and in silver and in gold exceedingly, and Lot, also, the son of his brother, was wealthy. 12. And Pharoah brought back Sara, the wife of Abram, and sent him out of the land of Egypt; and he came to a place where he had first fixed his tent, at the place of the altar at Age to the east of Bethel, and he went and blessed the Lord his God who had brought him back in peace. 13. And it happened in the forty-first jubilee, in the third year of the first week, he returned to this place, and placed upon it a burnt sacrifice, and called upon the name of the Lord, and said: "Thou, O Lord, Most High God, art my God to all eternity." 14. And in the fourth year of this week Lot separated from him, and Lot dwelt in Sodom; but the men of Sodom were great sinners. And he grieved in his heart that the son of his brother had separated from him, for he had no children. 15. And in that year when Lot was taken captive, the Lord also said to Abram, after Lot had separated from him, in the fourth year of this week, and said: "Lift up thine eyes from the place here where thou art dwelling toward the north and south and west and east. 16. For the whole land which thou seest I will give to thee and thy seed to eternity, and I will make thy seed like the sand on the sea; and when man is able to count the sand on the sea, then thy seed will be counted. 17. Arise and go through it in its length and breadth and see it all, for to thy seed I will give it." 18. And Abram went to Hebron and dwelt there. 19. And in that year came Kolodogomor, the king of Elam, and Emalphel, the king of Sinar, and Ariok, the king of Selasar, and Tirgal, the king of the Gentiles, and slew the king of Gomorrha, and the king of Sodom fled, and many fell by wounds in Sedemav and in the salt-district, and they took captive Sodom and Adam and Sheboem, and Lot, also, the son of the brother of Abram, and all his possessions, and went to Dan. 20. And one who had escaped came and told Abram, that the son of the brother of Abram had been taken captive. † 21. And the house-servant brought for Abram and his seed the first tenth to the Lord, and the Lord ordained it as an ordinance to eternity, that they should give (this) to

* Cf. Num. xiii. 22.

** I. e., עַיִן, **Taviv.** Num. xiii. 22.

† There is certainly a **lacuna** between this and the following verse, although there is nothing in the Ethiopic text to show it.

38

the priests who served before him, that they should possess it forever. 22. And to this law is not a limit of days, but it is ordained to the generation of eternity, that they should give the tenth to the Lord, of their seed and of their wine and of their oil and of their oxen and of their sheep. 23. And he gave it to his priests to eat and to drink in joy before him. 24. And the king of Sodom came to him and bowed down before him, and said: "Our lord Abram, give us the souls thou hast saved, but let the booty be thine." 25. And Abram said to him: "I lift up my hands to God on high, from a thread to a shoe-latchet I will take nothing from all that is thine, so that thou sayest not, 'I have made Abram rich,' only except what the youths have eaten and the portion for the men who came with me, Avnan, Eskol, and Mamre, these shall take their share."

CHAP. XIV. 1. And after these events, in the fourth year of this week, in the new moon of the third month, the voice of the Lord came to Abram in a dream, saying: "Fear not, Abram, for I am thy defender and thy exceeding great reward." 2. And he said: "O Lord, Lord, what wilt thou give me, and I have no son; and the son of Masek, the son of my maid-servant,* this Eleazer|of Damascus, will be my heir; but to me thou hast not given any seed." 3. And he said to him: "This one will not be thy heir, but he that comes from thy body, he will be thy heir." 4. And he took him without and said to him: "Look upon the heavens and see the stars of heaven, if thou art able to count them." 5. And he looked at the heavens and saw the stars; and he said to him: "Thus shall be thy seed." 6. And he believed the Lord, and it was accounted to him for righteousness. 7. And he said to him: "I am the Lord thy God, who have brought thee out of Ur of the Chaldees, that I might give thee the land of Canaan for an eternal possession, and I will be to thee and thy children after thee a God." 8. And he said: "O Lord, Lord, by what am I to know that I shall inherit it?" 9. And he said to him: "Take to thyself a heifer of three years, and a goat of three years, and a sheep of three years, and a turtle-dove and a pigeon." 10. And he took all these in the middle of the month, and he dwelt near the oak Mamre, which is near Hebron, and he built there an altar, and sacrificed all these and poured their blood upon the altar, and divided them into halves and laid them opposite each other; but the birds he did not divide. 12. And birds descended upon the pieces, and Abram drove them away and would not suffer the birds to touch them. 13. And it happened when the sun had set, a stupor fell upon Abram, and, behold, a great horror of darkness fell upon him, and it was spoken to Abram:** "Know in truth that thy seed will be a stranger in a strange land, and they will make them servants and oppress them four hundred years. 14. But the nation which they serve I will judge, and after that they will go out

* Cf LXX. on Gen. xv. 2.
** Cf. LXX. on Gen. xv. 13.

39

from there with many possessions. 15. And thou shalt go to thy fathers in peace and shalt be buried in a good age. 16. And in the fourth generation they shall return hither, for not yet are the sins of the Amorites completed." 17. And he awoke from his sleep, and he arose, and the sun had set, and there was a flame, and, behold, an oven was smoking, and a flame of fire passed through between the pieces. 18. And on that day the Lord made a covenant with Abram, saying: "To thy seed I will give this land from the river of Egypt unto the great river Euphrates, the Kenites and the Kenizzites and the Kadmonites and the Perizzites and the Rephaimites and the Ewites and the Amorites and the Canaanites and the Girgashites." 19. And Abram went and took up the pieces and the birds and the fruit and the drink offerings, and the fire devoured them. 20. And on that day we made a covenant with Abram according to the covenant which he had made in this month with Noah; and Abram renewed the festival and ordinance for himself unto eternity.* 21. And Abram rejoiced and told all these things to Sara, his wife, and he believed that he would have seed; but she did not bring forth. And Sara advised her husband Abram, and said to him: "Go in to Hagar, my Egyptian maid; it is possible that he will raise up for thee seed from her." 22. And Abram obeyed the voice of Sara, his wife, and said to her, "Do it," and Sara took her Egyptian maid Hagar and gave her to Abram, her husband, that she should become his wife. 23. And he went in to her, and she conceived and bore him a son, and he called his name Ishmael, in the fifth year of this week: and this was the eighty-sixth year of the life of Abram.**

CHAP. XV. 1. In the fifth year of the fourth week of this jubilee, in the third month, in the beginning of the month, Abram celebrated the festival of the first of the grain harvest; and he brought new offerings beside offerings of the first-fruits to the Lord, an ox and a goat and a sheep upon the altar as a sacrifice to the Lord, and their fruit offerings and their drink offerings he placed upon the altar together with frankincense. 2. And the Lord appeared to Abram and said to him: "I am the omnipotent God; be pleasing to me and be perfect, and I will establish my covenant between me and thee, and will increase thee exceedingly." 3. And Abram fell down on his face. 4. And the Lord spoke to him and said: "Behold my ordinance is with thee, and I will make thee the father of many nations, and thy name shall no longer be Abram, and thy name henceforth and to eternity shall be Abraham, for I will make thee a father of many nations, and I will make thee exceedingly great, and will cause nations and kings to proceed from thee. 5. And I will establish my covenant between me and thee and between thy seed after thee in their generations, as an ordinance of eternity, that I will be a God to thee and to thy seed

---

* Cf. note on Chap. vi. 15.

** Gen. xvi. 16.

after thee in their generations, (and I will give thee) the land where thou art a stranger, the land of Canaan, that thou shalt be ruler over it to eternity, and I will be their God." 6. And the Lord said to Abraham: "And thou, preserve my covenant, thou and thy seed after thee, and circumcise all your foreskins, and let it be a sign of my ordinance unto eternity between me and thee and for thy descendants. 7. On the eighth day ye shall circumcise all the males in your generation, the members of the household, and him whom ye have bought with gold from all the sons of the strangers whom ye have as your property, who are not of thy seed, — they shall circumcise the children of the household, and whomsoever ye have bought shall be circumcised. 8. And my covenant shall be on your flesh as an eternal ordinance; and whosoever is not circumcised on the eighth day, his soul shall be rooted out of his generation, for he has overthrown my covenant." 9. And the Lord said unto Abraham: "Sara, thy wife, shall no longer be called by her name Sara, for Sarah shall be her name;* for I will bless and give to thee a son from her, and I will bless him and he will become a people, and kings and nations shall proceed from him." 10. And Abraham fell upon his face and rejoiced, and he said in his heart: "Should there be born a son to one of a hundred years, and shall Sarah, who is ninety, yet bring forth!" 11. And Abraham said to the Lord: "O that Ishmael might live before thee!" 12. And the Lord said: "Yea, and Sarah also shall bear thee a son, and thou shalt call his name Isaac, and I will establish my eternal covenant with him and with his seed after him. 13. And also in reference to Ishmael have I heard thee, and, behold, I will bless him, and I will make him great and will increase him exceedingly, and twelve princes he will beget, and I will make him a great nation; but I will establish my covenant with Isaac, whom Sarah will bear for thee, in these days, in the second year." 14. And having ended speaking with him, the Lord ascended from over above Abraham. 15. And Abraham did as the Lord had said to him, and took Ishmael his son, and all the members of his household, and those whom he had bought with gold, all the males that were in his house, and circumcised the flesh of their sexual member. 16. And at the time of these days Abraham was circumcised, and all the men of his house and all whom he had bought with gold from among the sons of the strangers were circumcised with him. 17. And this is the law for all the generations of eternity, with no change of days and no deviation of day from the eighth day, for it is an eternal ordinance, ordained and written in the tablets of heaven. 18. And every one that is born, the flesh of whose member is not circumcised upon the eighth day, is not of the children of the

* The actual change made, according to the Ethiopic, is from Sora to Sara, which is the same as made in the best MSS. of the Ethiopic Bible in Gen. xvii. 15. Really, throughout the text, before this, the Book of Jubilees has been using the word Sora, for which now Sara is employed. In Ethiopic this involves no change in the meaning of the name. The LXX. changes from Σάρα to Σάῤῥα.

covenant which the Lord made with Abraham, but is of the children of destruction; and he has no sign upon him that he is the Lord's, but he is for destruction and slaying from the earth and for rooting out of the earth; for he has broken the covenant of the Lord our God. 19. For all the angels of the face and all the angels of glorification were thus created from the day of their creation;* and he looked upon the angels of glorification, and he sanctified Israel that they should be with him and with his holy angels. 20. And thou command the children of Israel and let them observe the sign of this covenant, and for their generations as an eternal ordinance that they be not rooted out of the land. 21. For it is ordained as a command of the covenant that they should observe it forever among all the children of Israel. 22. For Ishmael and his sons and his brothers and Esau the Lord did not permit to approach him and did not choose them, for the sons of Abraham are those he acknowledged, and he chose Israel to be his people. 23. And he sanctified it and collected it from among all the children of men, for there are many nations and many peoples, and all are his, and over all has he appointed spirits to rule, that they should lead them astray from him, but over Israel he did not appoint any ruler, neither an angel nor a spirit, but he alone is their ruler, and he preserves them, and he contends for them against the hands of his angels and his spirits and all; and they shall keep all his command-ments, and he will bless them, and they shall be his, and he will be theirs, from now on and to eternity. 24. And from now on I will announce to you that the children of Israel will break faith with this ordinance, and will not circumcise their sons according to this whole law, for they will omit this circumcision of the children on the flesh of their circumcision, and they all, the sons of Belial, will leave their children without circumcision as they were born. 25. And the wrath upon the children of Israel will be great from the Lord, for they have deserted his covenant, and have departed from his word, and enrage him and blaspheme him, as they do not observe this ordinance according to this sign, for they make their members like the Gentiles for being torn and rooted out of the land. And no longer is there forgiveness or pardon for them that all their sin may be forgiven and pardoned for this error to eternity.

CHAP. XVI. 1. And at the new moon of the fourth month we appeared to Abraham at the oak of Mamre, and we conversed with him, and we announced to him that a son would be given him from Sarah his wife. 2. And Sarah laughed, for she heard that we spoke these words with Abraham; and we admonished her, and she became afraid and denied that she had laughed on account of the words. 3. And we told her the name of her son as it is written on the tablets of heaven, namely, Isaac, as his name. 4. And when we returned to

* The angels even are circumcised, or rather created in that condition. One of the MSS. upon which D. bases his Ethiopic text omits this sentence.

her in a fixed time then she was pregnant with a son.   5. And in this month the Lord carried out the judgments of Sodom and Gomorrah and Sebruem and all the circuit of the Jordan, and burnt them with fire and brimstone, and demolished them unto the present day, according to what we have made known to thee concerning all their actions, that they were terrible and very sinful and have defiled themselves and committed fornication and uncleanness over the earth. 6. And accordingly the Lord inflicted judgment upon all the places by the hand of his servants, according to the uncleanness of Sodom, according to the judgment of Sodom.   7. But Lot we saved, for the Lord remembered Abraham, and led him out of the destruction. 8. And he and his daughters committed sin on the earth, such as had not been from the days of Adam until now, for the man lay with his daughters.   9. And, behold, it is commanded and engraven concerning all his seed on the tablets of heaven, that they should tear them out and root them out and judge them according to the judgment of Sodom, and that no seed should be left this man on the earth in the day of judgment.   10. And in this month Abraham migrated from Hebron, and dwelt between Kades and Shur in the mountains of Geraron.   11. And in the middle of the fifth month he migrated from there and dwelt at the well of the oath.* And in the middle of the sixth month the Lord visited Sarah, and did to her as he had said to her, and she conceived and bore a son.   And in the third month, in the middle of the month, in the days which the Lord had said to Abraham, on the festival of the first harvest, Isaac was born; and Abraham circumcised his son on the eighth day: he was the first one circumcised in the covenant as it was ordained forever.   12. And in the sixth year, in this month, of the fourth week, we came to Abraham to the well of the oath, and we appeared to him as we had told Sarah, that we would come to her, but she became pregnant with a son, and we returned in the seventh month and found Sarah pregnant before us, and we blessed her and told her all things that had been commanded us concerning him (Abraham) that he should not die until six sons had been born to him, and that he would see them before he should die: but that in Isaac his name and seed should be called.   13. And all the seed of his (other) sons will become Gentiles and will be numbered with the Gentiles; but from the sons of Isaac one shall become a holy seed and shall not be numbered among the Gentiles.   14. For he shall become the portion of the Most High, and among those of whom God is ruler will be his abode and all his seed, that it become a seed of the Lord, a nation of inheritance among all the nations, and that it may be a kingdom and a priesthood and a holy nation.   15. And we went our way, and we announced to Sarah all that we had told him; and these two rejoiced with an exceeding great joy.   16. And he built there an altar to the Lord who had saved him and had filled him with joy in the land of his pilgrimage, and he celebrated a festival of great

* I. e., Beer-Sheba.

43

joy in this month, seven days, at the altar which he had built at the fountain of the oath; and he built tents for himself and his servants on this festival, and he was the first one to celebrate the festival of tabernacles on the earth.   17. And in these seven days Abraham would bring every single day upon the altar a burnt offering to the Lord, two oxen, seven sheep, one young goat, on account of his sins that thereby these might be forgiven him and his seed, and as an offering of salvation seven rams, seven goats, and their fruit offering and their drink offering; over all the fat thereof he burnt incense upon the altar as a sacrifice chosen to the Lord as a sweet savor.   18. At mornings and evenings he burnt frankicense, galbanum, stakle and wood and myrrh and spice and costum; all these seven he brought, united with each other in equal parts and clean.   19. And thus he celebrated his festival seven days, rejoicing with his whole heart and his whole soul, he and all those that were in his house; and there was not any stranger with him nor any bastard.   20. And he blessed his Creator who had created him in his generation, for according to his pleasure did he create him; for he knew and observed that from him would come the plant of righteousness for the generations of eternity, and that from him should also come the holy seed, like him who had made all things.*   21. And he blessed his Creator, and he was glad, and he called the name of this festival the festival of the Lord with a joy acceptable to the Most High God.   22. And we blessed him forever and all his seed after him in all the generations of the world on this earth, because he celebrated this festival in its house according to the testimony of the tablets of heaven.   23. On this account it is ordained in the tablets of heaven concerning Israel that they shall celebrate the festival of the tabernacles seven days in joy, in the seventh month, that it be accepted before the Lord as an eternal law in the generations of all the years.   24. And to this there is no limit of days, but it is ordained over Israel as a festival that they shall observe it, and shall dwell in tents, and shall place wreaths upon their heads, and they shall take a willow branch with foliage from the brook.   25. And Abraham took the heart of the palm and good fruit of trees, and every day and day he would go around the altar with the branches, seven times a day, and in the morning he praised and thanked his God for all things in joy.

CHAP. XVII.   1. And in the first year of the fifth week Isaac was weaned, in this jubilee, and Abraham made a great feast in the third month on the day his son Isaac was weaned.   2. And Ishmael, the son of the Egyptian Hagar, was before the face of his father in this place; and Abraham rejoiced and blessed the Lord, because that he could see sons to himself and had not died without sons.   3. And he remembered the words which he had spoken to him on the day that Lot had separated from him; and he rejoiced, because the Lord had

* This is one of the passages in this book which can be interpreted messianically.

44

given him seed on the earth to inherit the land; and he blessed with his whole mouth the Creator of all things. 4. And when Sarah saw that Ishmael was playing and growing, and that Abraham was rejoicing exceedingly, she became jealous of Ishmael, and she said to Abraham: "Drive away this slave and her son, for the son of this one shall not inherit with my son Isaac." 5. And these words were grievous in the eyes of Abraham, on account of his maid, and on account of his son, that he should drive them away from him. 6. And the Lord said to Abraham: "Let it not be grievous in thy eyes concerning the child, concerning the slave; for in Isaac shall thy name and thy seed be called for thee. 7. But the son of this (slave) I will make into a great nation, for he is of thy seed. 8. And Abraham rose early in the morning and took bread and a bag of water and put them upon the shoulders of Hagar and of the boy and sent them away. 9. And she went wandering about in the desert Beer-Sheba; and the water was finished from the bag, and the boy was thirsty, and was not able to walk, and he fell down. 10. And his mother took him, and going, threw him under an olive tree, and she went and sat down opposite him, the distance of an arrow shot, saying: "I cannot see the death of my child;" and she sat weeping. 11. And an angel of God, one of the holy ones, said to Her: "Why dost thou weep, Hagar? Arising, take the boy, and lead him by the hand, for the Lord has heard thy voice." 12. And she looked at the bag and opened her eyes and saw a well of water, and she went and filled the bag with water and gave her boy to drink, and she arose and went toward the desert of Paran. 13. And the boy grew and became a horseman, and the Lord was with him. 14. And his mother took for him a wife from among the daughters of Egypt, and she bore him a son, and he called his name Nabemoth, for she said: "The Lord was near to me when I cried out to him." 15. And it happened in the seventh week, in the first year thereof, in the first month of this jubilee, on the twelfth of this month, there was a word in the heavens concerning Abraham, that he was a believer in all that the Lord told him, and that he loved him, because in all temptations he was faithful. 16. And the prince Mastema approached and said before God: "Behold Abraham loves Isaac his son, and esteems him more than all other things; say that he should bring him as a burnt offering on the altar and thou wilt see if he will do this word, and thou wilt know if he is a believer in everything with which thou triest him." 17. And the Lord knew that Abraham was a believer in all trials which he spoke to him; for he had tried him in his country, and in the strange land, and had tried him with the wealth of kings, and had tried him again with his wife in that she was torn from him, and with the circumcision, and had tried him with Ishmael and Hagar his maid, when he sent them away, and in all in which he had tried him he was found faithful, and his soul did not become impatient nor did he hesitate to do it, for he was faithful and a lover of God.

CHAP. XVIII. 1. And the Lord said to Abraham, "Abraham." And he said to him, "Behold, O Lord, here I am." 2. And he said to him: "Take thy son Isaac whom thou lovest, and go into the high land, and take him upon one of the hills which I will show thee." 3. And he arose in the morning from there and saddled his ass, and took two young men with him, and Isaac his son, and split the wood for a sacrifice, and he came to the place on the third day, and saw the place from afar. 4. And he came to a well of water, and he said to the young men: "Remain here with the ass, and I and the boy will go on and will worship, and after worshipping will return to you." 5. And he took the wood for the sacrifice and put it upon the shoulders of his son Isaac and he took in his hands the fire and the knife, and the two went together to that place. 6. And Isaac said to his father: "My father." 7. And he said to him: "Behold, here I am, my son." 8. (And he said) "Behold here is the fire, and the knife, and the wood; but where, my father, is the sheep for the sacrifice?" 9. And he said: "The Lord will show me the sheep for the sacrifice, my son." 10. And he came to the place of the hill of the Lord, and he built an altar and laid the wood upon the altar, and tied Isaac his son and placed him upon the wood over the altar, and he stretched out his hands to take the knife to sacrifice Isaac. 11. And I stood before him (God) and before the prince Mastema, and the Lord said: "Tell him not to lay his hand upon the boy and to do him no harm; for I know that he fears the Lord." 12. And the Lord called to him from heaven and said to him: "Abraham! Abraham!" and he was frightened and said: "Behold, here I am." 13. And he said to him: "Do not lay thy hands upon the boy, and do him no harm, for now I know that thou fearest the Lord, and hast not spared from me thy first-born son." 14. And the prince Mastema was confounded; and Abraham lifted up his eyes and looked, and behold a ram held fast with his horns. 15. And Abraham went and took the ram and brought him as a sacrifice in the place of his son Isaac. 16. And Abraham called this place "The Lord seeth," so that it is said "The Lord saw it" for Mount Zion.

17. And the Lord called Abraham by name a second time from heaven as he had appeared to us that we should speak to him in the name of the Lord. 18. And he said: "By my head, I swear, saith the Lord, because thou hast done this thing and hast not spared from me thy first-born son whom thou lovest, therefore I will surely bless thee and will surely increase thy head like the stars of heaven and like the sand of the shore of the sea. 19. And thy seed shall inherit the cities of their enemy, and in thy seed shall be blessed all the nations of the earth, for this that thou hast listened to my voice and hast shown unto all that thou art faithful unto me in all that I say to thee; go in peace." 20. And Abraham went to his young men, and they arose and went together to Beer-Sheba, and Abraham dwelt near the well of the oath; and he celebrated this festival in all the years, seven days

in joy, and called it "the festival of the Lord," according to the seven days in which he had gone and returned in peace. 21. And thus it is, and it is engraven and written in the tablets of heaven concerning Israel and its seed to keep this festival seven days in joy.

CHAP. XIX. 1. And in the first year of the first week in the forty-second jubilee Abraham returned and dwelt opposite Hebron, that is, Karjatarbok, two weeks of years. 2. And in the first year of the third week of this jubilee the days of the life of Sarah were completed, and she died in Hebron. 3. And Abraham went to mourn over and to bury her; and we tried him if his spirit was patient and if he was impatient in the words of his mouth, and he was found patient in this, and was not shaken. 4. For in the patience of his soul he conversed with the children of Keti that they should give him a place that he could bury his body in it; and the Lord gave him grace before all who saw him, and he asked with modesty of heart of the children of Keti, and they gave him the land of the double cave opposite Mamre, which is Hebron, for forty pieces of silver. 5. But they begged him, saying: "We will give it to thee;" and he did not take anything from them for nothing, for he gave the price for the place, perfect silver; and he bowed down before them twice, and then he buried the body in the double cave. 6. And all the days of the life of Sarah were one hundred and twenty-seven years, and this is two jubilees and four weeks and one year; those are the days of the years of the life of Sarah. And this was the tenth trial with which Abraham was tempted, and he was found faithful and of patient spirit. 8. And he did not speak a single word concerning that God had said that he would give him and his seed after him this land when he petitioned that he might bury his body there, for he was found faithful and patient and was written down as a friend of the Lord in the tablets of heaven. 9. And in the fourth year thereof he took a wife for Isaac his son, and her name was Rebecca, the daughter of Betuel, the son of Nahor, the brother of Abraham. 10. And Abraham took to himself a third wife, and her name was Keturah, from among the sons of his household, for Hagar had died before Sarah. 11. And she bore him six sons, Zambari, and Joksan, and Madai, and Ejazbok, and Sachai in the second week of years.* 12. And in the sixth week, in the second year, Rebecca bore to Isaac two sons, Jacob and Esau: but Jacob was pious and righteous and Esau was a rough man, a tiller of the field and hairy, but Jacob dwelt within tents. 13. And the youths grew, and Jacob learned writing; but Esau did not learn it, for he was a man of the field and a hunter, and learned war and all rough deeds. 14. But Abraham loved Jacob, but Isaac loved Esau. 15. And Abraham saw the deeds of Esau, and he knew that his name and seed should be called for him in Jacob, and he called Rebecca, and commanded her concerning

* Only five names are given in the Ethiopic text. The similarity of the names Medan and Midian (Gen. xxv. 2) has manifestly led to the ommission of one.

Jacob, for he saw that she too loved Jacob much more than Esau. 16. And he said to her: "My daughter, watch my son Jacob, for he shall be in my stead upon the earth as a blessing among the sons of men and to all the seed of Shem, and for an honor, and I know that the Lord has chosen him for himself as a people secluded from all those upon the face of the earth, and behold, Isaac, my son, loves Esau more than Jacob; add yet to do something good for him and let thine eyes be over him as the beloved, for he shall be to me a blessing over the earth, from now on and to all the generations of the earth. 17. Let thy hands be strong, and thou shalt rejoice in thy son Jacob, for him do I love exceedingly above all my children; for to eternity the Lord will be blessed in him, and his seed shall fill all the land. 18. If a man can number the dust of the earth then his seed will be numbered. 19. And all the blessings with which the Lord has blessed me and my seed shall be to Jacob and his seed all the days, and in his seed shall my name be blessed and the names of my fathers, Shem, and Noah, and Enoch, and Mahaalel, and Seth, and Adam; and these will serve to a founding of heaven and a strengthening of the earth and for a removal of all the stars upon the firmament."* 20. And he called Jacob before the eyes of his mother Rebecca, and he kissed him, and blessed him, and said to him; "My beloved son Jacob, whom my soul loveth, may God bless thee from the firmament above and give thee all the blessings with which he blessed Adam, and Enoch, and Noah, and Shem, and all that he has conversed with me and all that he has said that he would give me, may he fasten these to thee and to thy seed to eternity, according to the days of heaven over the earth. 21. And the spirits of Mastema shall not become masters over thee and over thy seed to remove thee from the Lord who is thy God, from now on and to eternity. 22. And may the Lord God be thy father, and thou his first-born son, and his people for all days: go, my son, in peace!" 23. And Rebecca loved Jacob with all her heart, and with all her soul, exceedingly more than Esau; and Isaac loved Esau exceedingly more than Jacob.

CHAP. XX. 1. And in the thirty-second jubilee, in the first year of the seventh week, Abraham called Ishmael and his twelve sons, and Isaac and his two sons, and the six sons of Keturah and their sons. 2. And he commanded them that they should preserve the path of the Lord to do righteousness and should love each his neighbor, and that they should be thus in all the wars that they go into against every one that is against them, and do justice and righteousness over the earth, and that they circumcise their sons according to the covenant which he had made with them, and that they should not transgress neither to the right hand nor to the left from all the paths which the Lord had commanded them, and that they should preserve themselves from all

---

* This probably means that a great nation is to come from Jacob, referring either to the Israel history or to that of the messianic period.

uncleanness, and that we should remove from our midst all uncleanness and fornication. 3. And if any woman or maid commit fornication among you, burn her with fire, and do not commit fornication after their eyes and hearts; and that they should not take unto themselves wives from among the daughters of Canaan, for the seed of Canaan shall be rooted out of the land. 4. And he spoke to them concerning the judgment of the giants and the judgment of Sodom, that these had been judged on account of their wickedness, and on account of fornication and uncleanness and destruction among each other. 5. "But be on your guard against all fornication and uncleanness and contamination of sin, so that ye do not make our name a curse and bring your lives and your sons to destruction by the sword and ye become accursed like Sodom, and all your remnant like the sons of Gomorrah. 6. And I call upon you as witnesses, my sons, love the God of heaven and submit to all his commandments, and do not walk after their idols and after their uncleanness, and do not make molten gods for yourselves nor wooden ones. 7. For they are vanity, and have no spirit, but they are the work of hands, and all who depend upon them . . . Do not worship them nor bow down to them. 8. But worship ye the Most High God and bow down to him ever, and hope upon his face at all times, and do rectitude and righteousness before him, that he may find pleasure in you and give you his mercy, and send down rain to you morning and evening, and bless all your work which ye do on the earth, and bless thy grain and thy water, and bless the seed of thy body, and the seed of thy land, and the herds of thy oxen, and the herds of thy sheep. 9. And thou shalt be for a blessing over the earth, and all the nations of the earth shall desire for you and will bless thy sons in my name that they be blessed as I am." 10. And he gave to Ishmael his son and to the sons of Keturah a gift and sent them away from Isaac his son. 11. And Ishmael and his sons and the sons of Keturah and their sons went together and dwelt from Pharmon (Pharan) to the entrance of Babylon, in all the land which faces toward the east opposite the desert. 12. And these mingled with each other, and their name was called Arabs and Ishmaelites.

CHAP. XXI. 1. And in the sixth year of the seventh week of this jubilee Abraham called Isaac his son, and his father commanded him saying: "I am gray and do not know the day of my death, for I am satisfied in my days. 2. And behold, my son, I am one hundred and seventy-five years old, and in all the days of my life I have ever remembered the Lord and sought with all my might that I might do the will of my God, and that I might walk aright in all his paths. 3. My soul hated idols so that I could be on my guard to do the will of him that created me, for he is the living God, and he is holy, and he is faithful, and he is just above all, and no evil is with him to have regard for persons and to take presents, for he is a god of righteousness, and a doer of judgment over all who transgress his commandments, and all that violate his covenant. 4. And thou, my son, observe his commandments and his ordinance and his judgment, and walk not after the unclean and after the wooden images and after the molten ones. 5. And do not eat any blood of an animal, or of a beast, or of any bird that flies in the heavens. 6. And if thou slaughterest, slaughter as a pure sacrifice that is acceptable; slaughter it and pour out its blood upon the altar and all the fat of the sacrifice place upon the altar with flour and fruit offering, mixed with oil together with drink offering, place all this together upon the altar as a sacrifice of sweet savor before the Lord. 7. Like the fat of the thank offering lay them upon the fire, like the fat of the belly, and all the fat upon the entrails, and the two kidneys and all the fat that is upon them, and upon the thigh pieces, and the liver, together with the kidneys wrapped up in them; bring this all as a sweet savor which will be acceptable before the Lord together with fruit and drink offerings, thou shalt bring them all together for a sweet savor as the bread of the burnt offering for the Lord. 7. And the meat eat on that day and on the second day, and do not let the sun go down on it on the second day until it is eaten and nothing shall be left over for the third day, for it is not acceptable nor chosen, and it shall no longer be eaten, and all who eat bring sin upon themselves. 8. For thus have I found it written in the books of my forefathers, in the words of Enoch and in the words of Noah. 9. And upon all thy sacrifices thou shalt put salt, and thou shalt not violate the covenant of salt in all thy sacrifices before the Lord. 10. And watch all the wood of the sacrifices, that thou dost not bring sacrificing wood beside the following: cypress, fir, and almond, and pine, and fir, and cedar, and savin, and citron, and olive, and myrrh, and balsam.* 11. Of these kinds of wood lay upon the altar, under the sacrifice, having examined its appearance, and do not place any broken or dark wood; hard wood and unbroken, perfect, and nearly grown, and not old, for its savor is gone and there is no more savor in it, as at first. 12. Besides these kinds of wood thou shalt place no other kinds, for its savor has departed, and thou shalt send up the smell of its savor to heaven. 13. Observe this commandment and do it, my son, that thou mayest be right in all thy actions. 14. And at all times be clean in thy body and wash thyself with water, before thou goest to sacrifice upon the altar, and wash thy hands and thy feet before thou approachest the altar; and when thou art done sacrificing, return and wash thy hands and thy feet. 15. And let there not appear upon any one of you any blood, nor upon your clothes: be on thy guard, my son, guard thyself exceedingly against blood; bury it in the ground. 16. And do not eat any blood for it is the soul, eat no blood whatever. 17. And do not receive any present for any blood of man that it should be spilt in vain without judgment, for this blood which is spilt causes sin upon the earth, and it cannot be cleansed of

---

* Cf. on these names Dillmann's Lexicon AEthiopico-Latinum.

the blood except by blood being shed; and do not receive a present or any gift for the blood of man; blood for blood; and ye shall become acceptable before the Lord God Most High, and he will be the protector of good, and that thou mayest be preserved from all evil and be saved from all death. 18. I see, my son, all the deeds of the sons of men, that they are sin and evil, and all their deeds are uncleanness, and rebellious and defiling, and there is no righteousness with them. 19. Guard thyself, do not go on their paths to step into their footprints and do not commit the error of death before the Most High God, lest he hide his face from thee, and return thee into the hands of thy transgression and root thee out of the land, and thy seed from under heaven, and thy name be destroyed and thy seed from all the earth. 20. Preserve thyself from all their deeds and from all their uncleanness, and observe the observance of the Lord Most High and do his will and do right in all things. 21. And he will bless thee in all thy deeds, and will bring forth from thee a plant of righteousness in all the earth, in all the generations of the earth. And my name shall be known, and thy name, under heaven, in all the days. 22. Go, my son, in peace. May the Most High God, my God and thy God, strengthen thee to do his will, and may he bless all thy seed and the descendants of thy seeds to the generations of eternity, with all the blessings of righteousness, that thou mayest be a blessing on all the earth." 23. And he went out from him, rejoicing happy.

CHAP. XXII. 1. And it happened in the first week of the forty-third (fourth) jubilee, in the second year, that is the year in which Abraham died, Isaac and Ishmael came from the fountain of the oath that they might celebrate the festival of the seven days, that is, the festival of the first-fruits of the harvest, with Abraham, their father; and Abraham rejoiced because his two sons came to him. 2. For Isaac had much possessions in Beer-Sheba, and Isaac went out to see his possessions and returned to his father. 3. And in these days Ishmael came to see his father, and they all came together, and Isaac offered up a sacrifice as a burnt offering, and brought it upon the altar which his father had made at Hebron. 4. And he offered a thank offering and made a feast of joy before his brother Ishmael, and Rebecca made new cakes out of new grain, and she gave thereof to Jacob, her best son, that he should bring to Abraham, his father, from the first-fruits of the land, that he might eat and bless the Creator of all before he died. 5. And Isaac, too, sent by the hand of Jacob, who excelled, a thank offering to Abraham, that he should drink and eat. 6. And he ate and drank and blessed the Most High God, who had created the heavens and the earth, and had made all the fat of the earth and had given it to the children of men to eat and to drink and that they should bless their Creator. 7. "And now I humbly thank thee, my Lord, that thou hast shown to me this day: behold, I am one hundred and seventy-five years old and full of days, and all the days were peace.

8. The sword of the hater did not overcome me in all that thou hast given me and my children all the days of my life until the present day. 9. My God, thy grace be over thy servant and over the seed of his sons, that he may be to thee a chosen nation and an inheritance from amongst all the nations of the earth, from now on and to all the days of the generations of the earth unto all eternities." 10. And he called Jacob and said to him: "My son Jacob, the Lord of all bless thee and strengthen thee to do righteousness and his will before him, and may he choose thee and thy seed that ye may be a people for his inheritance, according to his will in all the days. 11. And thou, my son Jacob, come hither and kiss me." 12. And he approached and kissed him, and he said: "Blessed be Jacob, my son, and all his children to the Lord Most High in all eternities; may the Lord give thee a seed of righteousness from among thy sons, to sanctify him in the midst of all the earth; and may all the nations serve and bow down to thy seed. 13. Become powerful before men, as thou rulest over all the seed of the earth and among the seed of Seth, when thy path and the path of thy sons is just for being his holy nation. 14. May the Most High God give thee all the blessings with which he blessed me and with which he blessed Noah and Adam; may they rest upon the sacred head of thy seed to all generations and to eternity. 15. And may the Lord preserve thee clean from all unclean defilement, that thou mayest be forgiven of all the sins which without knowledge thou hast committed, and may he strengthen thee and bless thee, and mayest thou inherit the whole earth. 16. And may he renew his covenant with thee, that thou mayest be to him a nation for his inheritance to all eternities, and he may be to thee and to thy seed a God in reality and in truth in all the days of the earth. 17. And thou, my son Jacob, remember my words and observe the commandments of Abraham, thy father; withdraw from among the Gentiles and do not eat with them, and do not according to their actions, and be not their companion; for their actions are unclean and all their ways are defiled and their sacrifices an abomination. 18. They sacrifice to the dead, and the evil spirits they worship, and in the graves they eat, and all their doings are in vain and for naught. 19. They have no heart to think and no eyes to see any of their actions and when they err, saying to a piece of wood, "Thou art my God," and to a stone, "Thou are my Lord and my saviour," and these have no heart. 20. And thou, my son Jacob, may the Most High Lord aid thee, and the God of heaven bless thee and preserve thee from all their uncleanness and from all their error. 21. Be thou on thy guard, my son Jacob, that thou takest not a wife from among all the seed of the daughters of Canaan, for all its seed is to be rooted out of the land; for on account of the sin of Ham and the transgression of Canaan also all his seed will be destroyed from the earth, and none will be left and escape of them on the day of judgment. 22. And all those that worship idols and all haters will have no hope in the land of the living, for they will descend into Sheol and will go unto the place

of judgment, and there will not be any remembrance of them on the earth; just as the children of Sodom were taken away from the earth, there will be taken away all those that worship idols. 23. Fear not, my son Jacob, and do not tremble, son of Abraham; the Most High God will protect thee from all destruction, and from all the paths of error he will deliver thee. 24. This house I have built for myself, that I might place my name above it upon the land which is given to thee and to thy seed forever, and that it should be called the house of Abraham; it is given to thee and to thy seed forever, since thou wilt build up my house and wilt establish my name before God unto eternity, and thy seed and thy name will stand in all the generations of the earth." 25. And he ceased speaking and commanding and blessing. 26. And the two lay together on one bed, and Jacob slept in the bosom of Abraham, the father of his father, and his thoughts kissed him seven times, and his love and his heart rejoiced over him. 27. And he blessed him with his whole heart and said: "The Most High God, the God of all, the Creator of all, who has led me out of Ur of the Chaldees, that he might give me this land as an inheritance to eternity and that I should establish a holy seed, may the Most High be blessed to eternity." 28. And he blessed Jacob and said: "My son, who is in all my heart and in all my thoughts, may I rejoice in him, and may thy grace and thy mercy be extensive over him and over his seed all the days. 29. And do not desert him and do not neglect him from now on and to the eternity of days, and may thy eyes be open over him and over his seed, that thou protectest him and blessest him and sanctifiest him, to be a nation for thy inheritance. 30. And bless him with all thy blessings from now on and to all the days to eternity, and renew thy covenant, and be merciful with him and with his seed, in all thy will to all the generations of the earth."

CHAP. XXIII. 1. And he laid two fingers of Jacob upon his eyes, and he blessed the God of gods, and he covered his face and stretched out his feet and slept the sleep of eternity and was gathered to his father. 2. And during all this, Jacob was lying on his bosom and did not know that Abraham, the father of his father, was dead. 3. And Jacob awoke from his sleep, and, behold, Abraham was cold like ice, and he said, "Father! father!" and no one answered, and he knew that Abraham was dead. 4. And he arose from his bosom and ran and told it to Rebecca, his mother, and Rebecca went to Isaac in the night and told him, and they went together and Jacob with them, and a lamp was in his hand, and going they found Abraham as a corpse. 5. And Isaac fell upon the face of his father Abraham, and wept and blessed him and kissed him; and the words were heard in the house of Abraham, and Ishmael, his son, arose and came to his father Abraham, and wept over Abraham, his father, he and all the house of Abraham, and they wept exceedingly. 6. And his sons Isaac and Ishmael buried him in the double cave, near to Sarah, his wife, and they mourned over him forty days, all the people of his house, Isaac and Ishmael and all their children and the children of Keturah in their places; and the lamentation and weeping over Abraham was ended. 7. And he lived three jubilees and four weeks of years, one hundred and seventy-five years, and the days of his life were completed, and he was old, perfect in days. 8. For the days of the lives of the first fathers were nineteen jubilees, and after the flood they began to decrease from nineteen jubilees, diminishing the jubilees and becoming speedily old and satisfying their days on account of the many sufferings and the wickedness of their ways, with the exception of Abraham. 9. But Abraham was perfect in his deeds with the Lord and well pleasing and in righteousness all the days of his life; and behold, he did not complete four jubilees in his life until he grew old on account of wickedness, and satisfied with days. 10. And all the generations that arise from then and unto the day of the great judgment age die speedily before completing two jubilees. 11. And it will be since their knowledge leaves them on account of their old age that also all their knowledge ceases. 12. And on that day if a man lives a jubilee and a half jubilee, they say concerning him, "He has lived long;" and the mass of his days are sufferings and pain and trouble and no peace, for punishment follows upon punishment, hostility upon hostility, trouble upon trouble, wickedness upon wickedness, sickness upon sickness, and all evil judgments of this kind, as sickness and' inflamation and hail and ice and snow and fever and suffering and becoming stiff, and sterility and death and sword and captivity and all the punishments and sufferings. 13. All this comes in the evil generation which sins upon the earth with the uncleanness of fornication and defilement and the abomination of their deeds. 14. And then they will say: "The days of the fathers were many, even to one thousand years, and were good, and behold the days of our lives, if a man has lived many, are seventy years, and if he is strong, eighty years, and all were evil and no peace will be in this evil generation." 15. And in that generation the children will be about to upbraid their fathers and their sires concerning the sin, and concerning the injustice and concerning the words of their mouth, and concerning the great wickedness which they do, and concerning their deserting the ordinances which the Lord had covenanted between them and him, that they should observe and do all his commandments and his ordinances and all his laws and not depart to the right or to the left. 16. For all are wicked, and every mouth speaks transgression, and all their deeds are unclean and an abomination, and all their paths are contamination and uncleanness and destruction. 17. Behold, the earth will be destroyed on account of all their deeds, and there will be no seed of wine and no oil, because all their deeds are unbelief, and they all will be destroyed together, the beasts and the animals and the birds and all the fish of the sea, on account of the sons of men. 18. And they will contend with each other, the young with the old and the old with the young; the poor with the rich, and the lowly with the great, and the beggar with the prince, on account of the law and on account of the covenant, for they have forgotten his commandments and his covenant and the festivals and the months and the sabbaths and the jubilees and all law.   19. And they will arise with swords and murder to bring them back to the path, but they will not return until the blood of many has been spilt upon the earth, one over the other.   20. And those who escape will not return on the path of righteousness from their wickedness, for they all will arise for a robbery for wealth, that each one may take that which is his neighbors' and be called by a great name, but not in reality and in truth, and the most holy will be defiled in the uncleanness of the destruction of their defilement. 21. And a great punishment will be over the deeds of this generation from the Lord, and he will give them over to the sword and to judgment and to captivity and to robbery and to devouring.   22. And he will awaken over them the sinners of the Gentiles, who will have no mercy or grace for them, and who regard the face of none, neither old nor young nor any one; for they are wicked and powerful that they act more wickedly than all the children of men; and in Israel they practise violence and sin in Jacob, and the blood of many will be spilt on the land; and there will be none to gather and to bury.   23. And in those days they will cry aloud and call and pray that they will be saved from the hands of the sinful Gentiles, and there will be none to save them.

24. And the heads of the children will be white with gray hair, and a child of three weeks will appear as old as a man of a hundred years, and their standing will be destroyed by trouble and oppression. 25. And in those days the children will begin to seek the laws and to seek the commandments and to return to the path of righteousness. 26. And the days will begin to increase and grow many, and the children of men generation by generation and day by day, until their days approach to one thousand years and to a multitude of years and days.   27. And no one will be old or satisfied with days, for all will be (like) children and youths.   28. And all their days will be in peace, and in joy they will end them and live, and there will be no satan nor any destroyer, for all their days will be days of peace and healings and blessings.   29. And at that time the Lord will heal his servants, and they will arise and see great peace and will cast out their enemies; and the just shall see it and be thankful and rejoice in joy to all eternity and shall see judgment and curses upon all their enemies.   30. And their bones shall rest in the earth, but their spirits shall increase in joy, and they shall know that the Lord is the doer of judgment, and gives mercy to the hundreds and thousands and to all that love him. 31. And thou, Moses, write down all these words, for thus are they written, and they have raised them upon the tablets of heaven to the generation of eternity.*

* Cf. Enoch c. 5 et passim.

CHAP. XXIV. 1. And it happened after the death of Abraham that the Lord blessed Isaac, his son, and he arose from Hebron and went and dwelt at the fountain of the vision, in the first year of the third week of this jubilee, seven years. 2. And in the first year of the fourth week a famine began in the land, in addition to the first famine which was in the days of Abraham. 3. And Jacob cooked a mess of lentils, and Esau came from the field hungry. 4. And he said to Jacob, his brother, "Give me of thy mess of pulse;" and Jacob said to him, "Give up to me thy right of first birth, and I will give thee bread and also from this mess of pulse." 5. And Esau said in his heart, "I shall die; what is it to me to be born first?" 6. And he said to Jacob, "I will give it to you." 7. And Jacob said, "Swear to me this day," and he swore to him. 8. And Jacob gave to his brother Esau bread and the mess, and he ate and was satisfied, and Esau despised his right of first birth; and from this was Esau called Edom,* on account of the mess of grain which Jacob gave him for his right of first birth. 9. And Jacob became the older, but Esau diminished from his greatness. 10. And the famine was over the land, and Isaac went to go down to Egypt in the second year of this week, and he went to the king of the Philistines at Gerara, to Abimelech. 11. And the Lord appeared to him and said to him: "Do not go down to Egypt; dwell in the land which I tell thee of: be a stranger in this land, and I will be with thee and will bless thee. 12. For to thee and to thy seed I will give all this land, and I will confirm my oath which I swore to Abraham, thy father, and I will increase thy seed like the stars of the heavens, and I will give to thy seed all this land. 13. And in thy seed shall be blessed all the nations of the earth, because thy father hearkened unto my voice and observed my words and my commandments and my law and my ordinances and my covenant; and now hear my voice and dwell in this land." 14. And he dwelt at Gerar three weeks of years. 15. And Abimelech commanded on his account and on account of all that was his, saying: "Every man that touches him or any thing that is his, shall surely die." 16. And Isaac increased in Philistia, and he secured many possessions, oxen and sheep and camels and asses and many possessions. 17. And he sowed in the land of Philistia and he raised a hundred-fold, and Isaac became exceedingly great, and the Philistines were jealous of him, and all the wells which the young men of Abraham had dug during the life of Abraham the Philistines covered after the death of Abraham and filled them with earth. 18. And Abimelech said to Isaac: "Go from me, for thou art exceedingly greater than I;" and Isaac went in the first year of this seventh week from there, and migrated to valleys of Geranon. 19. And they returned and dug open the wells of water, which the servants of Abraham, his father, had dug, and which the Philistines had covered over after the death of Abraham, his father, and he called

* The Ethiopic translator must have read ἐψήματος πυροῦ for πυρροῦ. Cf. LXX. on Gen. xxv. 30.

their names as Abraham, his father, had named them. 20. And the young men of Isaac dug wells in the valley, and found living water; and the shepherds of Geranon quarrelled with the shepherds of Isaac, saying, "This is our water," and Isaac called the name of this well Contention, "because ye have contended with us." 21. And they dug another well, and quarrelled on its account, and Isaac called its name Narrowness. 22. And he arose from there, and they dug another well, and did not quarrel on its account, and he called its name Extension, and Isaac said, "Now the Lord has extended us;" and he increased in the land. 23. And he ascended from there to the well of the oath in the first year of the first week in the forty-third jubilee. 24. And the Lord appeared to him in this night, at the new moon of the first month, and said to him: "I am the God of Abraham, thy father: fear not, for I am with thee, and I will bless thee and increase thy seed like the sand of the sea, on account of Abraham, my servant." 25. And he built an altar there where Abraham, his father, had first built one, and he called upon the name of the Lord, and offered sacrifices to the God of Abraham, his father. And they dug a well and found living water. 26. And the young men of Isaac dug another well, and did not find water, and they went and told Isaac that they had not found water, and Isaac said: "I have sworn this day to the Philistines, and this is to us the affair." 27. And Isaac called the name of this place The Well of the Oath, for there had he sworn to Abimelech and Akosat, his friend, and Phikol his companion. 28. And Isaac knew on that day that in injustice they had sworn to them to keep the peace with them. 29. And Isaac on that day cursed the Philistines, and he said: "Cursed be the Philistines to the day of wrath and rage above all nations: may the Lord make them an ignominy and a curse and anger and rage in the hands of sinful nations, and by the hands of the Hittites let him root them out. 30. And whoever escapes from the sword of the enemy and from the Hittites, may the people of the just root them out in judgment from under heaven, for they will be enemies and haters to my children in their days over the earth. 31. And may no remnant them be left nor may any be saved on the day of the judgment of wrath, for to destruction and rooting out and being destroyed from the land are all the seed of the Philistines, and no remnant or name shall be left of **their** seed over the earth. 32. For even if he had ascended to heaven, they would bring him down from there; and if he is fortified upon the earth they will tear him from there; and if he hides himself among the Gentiles, they will destroy him from there; and even if he descends into Sheol, there too shall his judgment be great, and no peace shall be to him; and if he go into captivity, by the hand of those that seek his soul on the way he shall be killed, and no name or seed shall be left him on the whole earth, for he shall go into the curse of eternity." 33. And thus is it written and engraved concerning him on the tablets of heaven, to do to him on the day of judgment, that he may be rooted out of the earth.

CHAP. XXV. 1. And in the second year of this week in this jubilee Rebecca called Jacob her son, and spake to him, saying: "My son, do not take to thyself a wife from among the daughters of Canaan, like Esau, thy brother, who took to himself as wives two from the seed of Canaan, and they embittered my spirit with all their unclean deeds, for all their deeds are fornication and shame, and there is no righteousness in them, but it is evil. 2. And I, my son, love thee exceedingly, and my mercy, my son, blesses thee at every hour and watch of the night; and now, my son, hear my voice, and do the will of thy mother, and do not take to thyself a wife from among the daughters of this land, except from the house of thy father and except from the family of thy father: take to thyself a wife from the house of my father, and the Most High God will bless thee, and thy children will be a generation of righteousness and thy seed holy." 3. And then spake Jacob with his mother Rebecca, and said to her: "Behold, I am now nine weeks of years old and know no woman: I have touched none nor betrothed myself to any, nor do I think of Taking to myself a wife from all the seed of the daughters of Canaan. 4. For I remember, O mother, the words of Abraham, our father, that he commanded me not to take my wife from among all the seed of the house of Canaan, but from the seed of my father's house I should take to myself a wife and from my relationship. 5. I have heard before that daughters have been born to Laban, thy brother, and upon them is my heart set to take a wife of them. 6. On this account I have preserved myself in my spirit not to sin nor defile myself in all my ways all the days of my life, for with reference to lust and fornication my father Abraham gave me many commands. 7. And with all that he has commanded me these twenty-two years my brother contends with me and continually converses, saying: My brother, take to wife one of the sisters of my two wives; but I am not willing to do as my brother has done. 8. I swear before thee, my mother, that all the days of my life I will not take to myself a wife from the seed of all the daughters of Canaan, and will not act wickedly as my brother has done. 9. And do not fear, mother; trust me that I will do thy will, and will walk in rectitude, and my paths will not be destroyed in eternity." 10. And then she lifted up her face to heaven and extended the fingers of her hand to heaven, and opened her mouth and blessed the Most High God, who had created heaven and earth, and she gave him thanks and praise. 11. And she said: "Blessed be the Lord God and blessed be his name for ever and ever, who has given to me Jacob as a pure son and a holy seed; for thine he is and thine shall be his seed unto all the days and in all the generations of the world. 12. Bless him, O Lord, and place the blessing of righteousness in my mouth that I may bless him." 13. And at that hour the Holy Spirit descended into her mouth, and she placed her two hands upon the head of Jacob, and she said: "Blessed art thou, Lord of righteousness and God of the worlds, and thee do all the generations of men praise: may he give thee, my son, the path of righteousness, and reveal to thy seed righteousness. 14. And may thy sons increase in thy life, and stand to the number of the months of the year, and may thy sons increase and grow more than the stars of the heavens, and more than the sand of the sea increase their numbers. 15. And may he give to them this fruitful land, as he said he would give it to Abraham and his seed after him in all the days, and may they possess it to eternity. 16. And may I see for thee, my son, blessed children in this life, and may holy seed be all thy seed. 17. And as the spirit of thy mother in her life caused thee to rest in her womb to give thee birth, thus my affection blesses thee, and my breasts bless thee and my mouth and my tongue praise thee. 18. Increase and be poured over the earth, and thy seed be perfect in all the earth in the joy of heaven and earth, and may thy seed rejoice and on the great day of peace may the peace of thy name be theirs. 19. And may thy seed abide to all the worlds, and may the Most High God be their God, and may the Most High God dwell with them and his sanctuary be built to all the eternities. 20. He that blesses thee be blessed, and all flesh that curses thee in lies, may it be cursed." 21. And she kissed him and said to him, "May the Lord of the world love thee as the heart of thy mother, and may her affection rejoice in thee and bless thee." 22. And she ceased from blessing him.

CHAP. XXVI. 1. And in the seventh year of this week Isaac called Esau, his elder son, and said to him: "My son, I am old, and behold my eyes are dull of seeing, and I do not know the day of my death. 2. And now take thy hunting weapon and thy bow and thy quiver, and go to the field and hunt and catch something for me, my son, and prepare me a meal such as my soul loves, and bring it to me, so that I may eat and my soul bless thee before I die." 3. But Rebecca heard Isaac speaking to Esau. 4. And Esau went early to the field to hunt and catch something and bring it to his father. 5. And Rebecca called Jacob, her son, and said to him: "Behold, I have heard thy father Isaac speaking with thy brother Esau, saying, 'Hunt me something and prepare a meal and bring it in to me, and I will bless thee before the Lord before I die.' 6. But now hear, my son, my words which I command thee: Go to thy flocks and bring me two good young kids, and I will make a meal out of them such as he loves, and thou shalt bring it in to thy father and he shall eat, that he may bless thee before the Lord before he dies, and thou become blessed." 7. And Jacob said to his mother Rebecca: "O mother, I will not hold back anything that my father may eat and is pleasing to him; only I fear, my mother, that he will know my voice and will desire to touch me; and thou knowest that I am smooth, but my brother Esau is rough, and I may be before his eyes like an evil-doer, and I should do a deed which he has not commanded me, and he might become angry with me and I should bring a curse upon myself and not a blessing." 8. And

Rebecca, his mother, said to him: "Upon me, my son, be thy curse; and again listen to my voice." 9. And Jacob obeyed the words of his mother Rebecca, and he went and took two good and fat young kids and brought them in to his mother, and his mother made a meal out of them as he like it. 10. And Rebecca took the clothing of her elder son Esau, the most precious with her in the house, and clothed Jacob with them, and the skins of kids she placed over his hands and upon the exposed parts of his body; and she gave the meat and the bread which she had made into the hands of her son Jacob. 11. And he went in to his father and said: "Behold, I am thy son; I have done as thou hast said to me: arise and sit up and eat of what I have hunted, my father, that thy soul may bless me." 12. And Isaac said to his son, "What is this, that thou hast so suddenly found it, my son?" 13. And Jacob said to him: "He who has caused me to find it, thy God, is before me." 14. And Isaac said: "Come hither to me, that I may touch thee, my son, if thou art my son Esau, or if not." 15. And Jacob came near to Isaac his father, and he touched him. 16. And he said: "The voice is the voice of Jacob, but the hand is the hand of Esau;" and he did not know him, for it was a fate from heaven to remove his spirit; and Isaac did not know him, for his hands were like his (i. e., Esau's) hands, and hairy like the hands of Esau, so that he should bless him. 17. And he said, "Art thou my son Esau?" And he said, "I am thy son." And he said: "Bring hither to me, and I will eat of what thou hast hunted, my son, that my soul may bless thee." 18. And he brought to him the meal, and he ate; and he brought in wine, and he drank. 19. And Isaac, his father, said to him: "Approach and kiss me, my son;" and he approached and kissed him. 20. And he smelt the smell of his clothes, and he blessed him, and said: "Behold, the smell of my son is like the smell of the field which the Lord has blessed; and may the Lord give thee and increase thee like the dew of the heaven and the dew of earth, and may grain increase and oil be plenty to thee, and may the nations serve thee and the peoples bow down to thee. 21. Be the lord of thy brother, and may the sons of thy mother bow down to thee, and may all the blessings with which the Lord has blessed me and has blessed my father Abraham be thine and thy seed's to eternity: he that curseth thee shall be cursed, and he that blesseth thee shall be blessed." 22. And when Isaac ended blessing his son Jacob, then Jacob went out from Isaac his father to hide himself. 23. But Esau, his brother, came in from hunting, and said to his father, "Arise, my father, and eat of my prey, that thy soul may bless me." 24. And Isaac, his father, said to him, "Who art thou?" 25. And he said to him, "I am thy first-born son Esau; I have done as thou hast commanded me." 26. And Isaac was very much astounded, and said: "Who was he that hunted and caught something for me, and brought it in, and I ate of all before thou camest in, and I blessed him? 27. Blessed shall he be and his seed to eternity." 28. And when Esau heard the words of his father Isaac he cried with a loud and very bitter voice, and said to his father: "Bless me too, father!"   29. And he said to him, "Thy brother came and took thy blessing."   30. (And Esau said:) "And now I know why his name is called Jacob; behold he has ensnared me twice; the first time he took my birth-right, and now he takes my blessing.   31. And he said, "Hast thou not a blessing left for me, my father?"   32. And Isaac answered and said to Esau: "Behold, I have set him as lord over thee and all his brothers, and have given to them to be his servants, and with much grain and oil and wine I have strengthened him, and what shall I do to thee, my son?"   33. And Esau said to his father Isaac: "Hast thou but one blessing, father? Bless also me, father."   34. And Esau raised his voice and wept. And Isaac answered and said to him: "Behold, from the fatness of the earth shall be thy substance and from the dew of heaven above; and thou shalt live by thy sword and thou shalt serve thy brother.   35. And it will happen when thou art great and shalt break his yoke off thy neck, thou shalt commit a sin unto death, and all thy seed shall be rooted out from under heaven."   36. And Esau was wroth at Jacob on account of the blessing with which his father had blessed him; and he said in his heart, "Now the days of grief may come for my father, that I may kill my brother Jacob."

CHAP. XXVII.   1. And the words of Esau, her elder son, were told to Rebecca in a dream, and Rebecca, sending, called for Jacob, her younger son.   2. And she said to him: "Behold, thy brother Esau is making his plans to kill thee; and now hear my words: arise and flee to my brother Laban and dwell with him a number of days, until the anger of thy brother has turned and his anger has departed from thee and he forget every thing that thou hast done him, and I will send to bring thee from there."   3. And Jacob said: "I have no fear: if he desires to kill me, I will kill him."   4. And she said to him, "Then should I be deprived of both my sons in one day."   5. And Jacob said to his mother Rebecca: "Behold, thou knowest that my father is old, and I see that his eyes have become dull, and if I leave him it will be evil in his eyes that I leave him and go away from thee, and my father will be angry and curse me. I will not go; only if he sends me will I go from here."   6. and Rebecca said to Jacob: "I will go in and will speak to him, and he will send thee."   7. And Rebecca went in and spake to Isaac: "I am aggrieved in my life on account of the two daughters of Heth which Esau has taken to himself as wives from among the daughters of Canaan: why should I yet live? for the daughters of the land of Canaan are evil."   8. And Isaac called his son Jacob, and blessed him, and admonished him, and said to him: "Do not take to thee a wife from among all the daughters of Canaan; arise and go to Mesopotamia, to the house of the father of thy mother, to the house of Bethuel, and take to thee from there a wife from among the daughters of Laban, the brother of thy mother. And may the God of heaven bless thee and increase and enlarge thee, and become thou a collection of nations, and may he give the blessings of thy father Abraham to thee and thy seed after thee, that thou mayest inherit the land of thy pilgrimage and all the land which the Lord gave to Abraham: go, my son, in peace!" 9. And Isaac sent away Jacob, and he went to Mesopotamia to Laban, the son of Bethuel, the Syrian, the brother of Rebecca, the mother of Jacob. 10. And it happened when Jacob had arisen to go to Mesopotamia, the spirit of Rebecca was sad after her son had gone, and she wept. 11. And Isaac said to Rebecca: "My sister, weep not on account of Jacob, my son, for he is going in peace, and in peace he will return. 12. The Most High God will presserve him from all evil and will be with him, for he will not desert him any day of his life, for I perceive that the Lord will prosper his path wherever he goes, until he returns in peace to us and we see him in peace. 13. Do not fear on his account, my sister, for right is his path and he is a perfect and faithful man and will not be destroyed: do not weep!" 14. And Isaac comforted Rebecca on account of Jacob her son, and blessed him. 15. And Jacob went from The Well of the Oath that he might come to Haran in the first year of the second week in the forty-fourth jubilee, and came to Loza among the mountains, that is, Bethel, in the beginning of the first month of this week, and he came to the place at eve, and he turned off from the way toward the west from the highway in this night, and slept there, for the sun had set. 16 And he took one from among the stones of that place and laid it under a tree, and he was travelling alone, and he slept. 17. And he dreamed in that night a dream, and behold, a ladder was planted upon the earth, and its head reached to the heaven, and behold, the angels of the Lord ascended and descended on it, and behold, the Lord stood upon it. 18. And the Lord spake unto Jacob and said: "I am the Lord God of Abraham, thy father, and the God of Isaac: the land upon which thou art sleeping I will give to thee and to thy seed after thee, and thy seed shall be like the sand of the sea, and thou shalt increase to the west and east and south and north; and all the countries of the nations shall be blessed in thee and in thy seed. 19. And behold, I will be with thee and still watch over thee in all things wherever thou goest, and will bring thee back into this land in peace: for I will not leave thee until I do all that I have said to thee." 20. And Jacob finished his sleep, and said: "Truly this place is the house of the Lord, and I did not know it." 21. And he was afraid, and said: "Dreadful is this place, which is nothing but the house of the Lord, and this is the portal of heaven." 22. And Jacob awoke early in the morning and took the stone from under his head and placed it up as a pillar, as a sign of this place; and he poured oil upon its head, and called the name of this place Bethel; but its first name was Loza, like the land. 23. And Jacob prayed a prayer to the Lord, saying: "If the Lord will be with me and guard me on this path upon which I walk, and if the Lord give me bread to eat and clothes to clothe myself, and I return in peace to the house of my father, then the Lord shall be my God, and this stone, which I have set up as a pillar, as a sign in this place, shall be a house of the Lord.   24. And all things that thou givest me, of that I will give the tenth to thee, my God."

CHAP. XXVIII.   1. And he lifted up his feet and went to the land of the east, to Laban, the brother of his mother Rebecca, and he was with him and served him for Rachel, his daughter, one week. And in the first year of the third week he said to him: "Give me my wife, for whom I have served thee seven years."   2. And Laban said to Jacob, "I will give thee thy wife." And Laban made a feast, and took Leah, his older daughter, and gave her to Jacob as a wife, and gave her Zalapha as a maid to serve her; and Jacob did not know it, for he thought she was Rachel.   3. And he went in to her, and behold, it was Leah; and Jacob was angry at Laban and said to him: "Why hast thou done thus?   4. Have I not served thee for Rachel and not for Leah? Why hast thou injured me? Take thy daughter and I will go; for thou hast done evil to me."   5. For Jacob loved Rachel more than Leah, for the eyes of Leah were dull, but her form was very beautiful; but Rachel had beautiful eyes and a beautiful and very attractive form. 6. And Laban said to Jacob: "It is not the custom in our land to give the younger before the elder."   7. And it is not right to do this, for thus is it ordained and written on the tablets of heaven, that no one shall give his younger daughter before the older, but shall give the younger after her.   8. And the man that does this loads sin upon himself on this account in heaven, and no one who does this is just, for it is an evil deed before the Lord.   9. And thou command the children of Israel that they do not this thing, and neither take nor give the younger before the older has been established, for it is very wicked.   10. And Laban said to Jacob: "Let the seven days of this feast pass by, and I will give thee Rachel that thou mayest serve me another seven years, that thou mayest herd my sheep, as thou hast done in the first week."   11. And on the day when the seven days of the feast of Leah were passed, Laban gave Rachel to Jacob, that he might serve him a second seven years, and he gave Rachel Balla, the sister of Zalapha, as a maid to serve her.   12. And he served seven years again for Rachel, for Leah had been given to him.   13. And the Lord opened the womb of Leah, and she became pregnant and bore Jacob a son, and he called his name Reuben, on the fourteenth of the ninth month of the first year of the third week.   14. But the womb of Rachel was closed, for the Lord saw that Leah was hated but Rachel was beloved. 15. And again Jacob went in to Leah, and she conceived and bore Jacob a second son, and he called his name Simeon, on the twenty-first of the tenth month and the third year of this week.   16. And again Jacob went in to Leah, and she became pregnant and bore him a third son, and he called his name Levi, in the beginning of the third month, in the sixth year of this week.   17. And again Jacob went in to Leah, and she became pregnant and bore him a fourth son, and he called his name Judah, on the fifteenth of the third month in the first year of the fourth week.   18. And in all this Rachel was jealous of Leah, for she did not bear; and she said to Jacob, "Give me a son!'   19. And Jacob said to her, "Am I preventing fruit of the womb from thee: have I left thee?"   20. And when Rachel saw that Leah had borne Jacob four sons, Reuben, Simeon, Levi, and Judah, then she said to him, "Go in to Balla, my maid, and she will conceive and bear a son for me."   21. And he went in to her, and she became pregnant and bore him a son, and she called his name Dan, on the ninth of the sixth month, in the sixth year of the third week.   22. And again a second time he went in to Balla, and she became pregnant and bore Jacob another son, and Rachel called his name Naphtalim, in the fifth of the seventh month of the second year of the fourth week.   23. And when Leah saw that she had become sterile and did not bear, she became jealous of Rachel, and she gave Zalapha, her maid, to Jacob as a wife, and she became pregnant and bore him a son, and she called his name Gad, on the twelfth of the eighth month in the third year of the fourth week.   24. And again he went in to her, and she became pregnant and bore him another son, and Leah called his name Asher, on the second of the eleventh month in the fifth year of the fourth week.   25. And Jacob went in to Leah, and she became pregnant and bore Jacob a son, and she called his name Issachar, on the fourth of the fifth month in the fourth year of the fourth week, and she gave him to a nurse.   26. And Jacob again went in to her, and she became pregnant and she bore him two (children), a son and a daughter, and she called his name Zebulon and the name of the daughter Dinah, on the seventh of the seventh month in the sixth year of the fourth week.   27. And the Lord was gracious to Rachel and opened her womb, and she became pregnant and bore a son, and she called his name Joseph, in the beginning of the fourth month of the sixth year of this fourth week.   28. And in the days when Joseph was born Jacob said to Laban: "Give me my wives and my children, and I will go to my father Isaac, and I will make for myself a house, for I have completed the years which I have served thee for thy two daughters, and I will go to the house of my father."   29. And Laban said to Jacob: "Remain with me for wages, and herd my folds again and receive thy wages."   30. And they agreed with each other, that he would give him as wages all the young sheep and goats . . .should be his wages. And the possessions of Jacob increased very much, and he possessed oxen and sheep and asses and camels and sons and daughters.   31. And Laban and his sons were jealous of Jacob, and Laban gathered his sheep away from him, and thought out evil.

CHAP. XXIX.   1. And it happened when Rachel had given birth to Joseph that Laban went out to shear his sheep, for they were distant from him a journey of three days. 2. And Jacob saw that Laban had gone to shear his sheep, and he called Leah and Rachel, and spake unto their hearts, that they should go with him to the land of Canaan, for he told them all that he had seen in the dream, and all that he (God) had spoken to him, that he should return to the house of his father; and they said to him: "We will go everywhere thou goest, with thee we will go." 3. And Jacob blessed the God of his father Isaac, and the God of Abraham, the father of his father, and he arose and prepared his wives and children, and took all his possessions and crossed the river and came to the land of Gilead, and Jacob hid his heart from Laban and did not tell him. 4. And in the seventh year of the fourth week Jacob returned to Gilead in the first month, on the twenty-first; and Laban followed after him, and found Jacob in the mountains of Gilead, in the third month, on the twelfth thereof. 5. And the Lord did not permit him to injure Jacob, for he appeared to him in a dream by night; and Laban spake to Jacob. 6. And on the fifteenth thereof, on that day, Jacob made a feast to Laban and all who had come with him, and Jacob swore to Laban on this day and Laban to Jacob, that they would not cross for evil to one another the mountains of Gilead. 7. And he made there a large stone heap as a testimony; on this account the name of this place is called "The Stone Heap of Testimony;" such is the heap. 8. But before they had called the land of Gilead the land of Raphaim, for it was the land of the Raphaim, and the Raphaim, or giants, were born there, whose length is ten, nine, eight, and seven ells, and their dwellings were from the land of the sons of Ammon to Mount Hermon, and the seats of their kingdom were Koronaem and Adra and Misur and Beon. 9. And the Lord slew them on account of the wickedness of their deeds, for they were most terrible, and the Ammorites inhabit it in their place, evil and sinful, and there is no nation to-day that has completed all their sin, and therefore they have no length of life upon the earth. 10. And Jacob sent Laban away, and he came into the land of Mesopotamia, the land of the east, but Jacob returned to the land of Gilead and crossed over the Jabbok in the ninth month on the eleventh thereof. 11. And on that day Esau, his brother, came to him, and they settled their troubles; and they went from here into the land of Seir, but Jacob dwelt in tents. 12. And in the first year of the fifth week of this jubilee he crossed the Jordan and lived opposite the Jordan, that he might pasture his sheep from the land of Stone Heap to Beta-Zon and to Dotaem and to Akrabil. 13. And he sent to his father Isaac of all his possessions clothing and food and meat and drink and milk and oil and bread of milk and of the palms of the valley; and to his mother Rebecca he also sent four times a year, between the times of the months, between the plowing and the harvest, between the spring and the rain, and between winter and summer, to the tower of Abraham, for Isaac had returned from The Well of the Oath and had gone up to the tower of his father Abraham, and he dwelt there apart from his son Esau.   14. For in the days when Jacob went to Mesopotamia, Esau took to himself as wife Malit, the daughter of Ishmael, and collected all the herds of his father and his wives and went up and dwelt in the mountains of Seir, and left Isaac, his father, at The Well of the Oath alone; and Isaac went up from The Well of the Oath, and dwelt in the tower of Abraham, his father, on the mountains of Hebron.   15. And from here Jacob sent all things which he sent to his father Isaac and to his mother from time to time . . . all their sorrows; and they blessed Jacob with all their heart and all their souls.

CHAP. XXX.   1. And in the first year of the sixth week he went up to Salem, which is opposite the east of Shechem, in peace, in the fourth month; and there they brought by force Dinah, the daughter of Jacob, into the house of Shechem, the son of Hamor, the Hivite prince of the land, and he slept with her and defiled her, and she was a small girl twelve years of age.   2. And he begged her father and her brothers for her, that she should be given to him as wife; and Jacob and his sons were angry on account of the men of Shechem, because they had defiled their sister Dinah; and they spoke with them for evil, and intrigued against and deceived them.   3. And Simeon and Levi secretly came to Shechem and inflicted punishment upon all the men of Shechem, and slew all the men they found in it, and did not leave a single one in it.   4. They killed all in torments, because they had dishonored their sister Dinah.   5. And thus ye shall not do from now on and to eternity to defile a daughter of Israel, for in heaven it was ordained over them as a punishment that they should root out all the men of Shechem, because they committed a shame on a daughter of Israel, and the Lord turned them over into the hands of the sons of Jacob, that they should root them out with the sword, and that they should inflict punishment upon them; and never again shall it be thus in Israel, that a daughter of Israel be defiled.   6. And if there is any man in Israel who desires to give his daughter or his sister to any man who is of the seed of the Gentiles, he shall surely die, and they shall slay him with stones, for he has committed a sin and a shame in Israel; and his wife they shall burn with fire, for she has defiled the name of the house of her father, and she shall be rooted out of Israel.   7. And no fornication or defilement shall be found in Israel all the generations of the earth; for Israel is holy to the Lord, and every man that defiles must surely die, and they shall slay him with stones.   8. For thus it is ordained and written on the tablets of heaven concerning all the seed of Israel, that he who defiles must surely die, and they shall slay him with stones.   9. And to this law there is no limit of days and no ceasing and no forgiveness, but he shall be rooted out who defiles his daughter, among all Israel, because he has given of his seed to Moloch and has sinned by defiling.   10. And thou, Moses, command the children of Israel and testify over them that they shall not give any of their daughters to the Gentiles and that they shall not take any of the daughters of the Gentiles; for this is accursed before the Lord. 11. And on this account I have written for thee in the words of the law all the deeds of Shechem which they did against Dinah, and how the children of Jacob conversed saying: "We will not give our daughter to an uncircumcised man, for this is disgraceful to us." 12. And it is disgraceful to Israel to those that give and to those that receive from any Gentiles any daughters, for it is unclean and accursed to Israel; and Israel will not be clean of this uncleanness of him who has of the daughters of the Gentiles for a wife, or who has given of his daughters to a man who is of any of the seed of the Gentiles; for there will be plagues upon plagues, curse upon curse, and all punishment and plagues and curses will come. 13. And if they do this thing, and if they blind their eyes to those that commit uncleanness and to those that defile the sanctuary of the Lord and those that profane his holy name, then shall the whole people together be punished, on account of all this uncleanness and this profaneness, and there will be no respect for persons, and no consideration for persons, and no taking of fruits from his hands and fruit offering and burnt offering and fat and incense offering as a sweet savour, that it may be acceptable. 14. And every man and woman in Israel who defiles the sanctuary shall be thus. 15. And on account of this I have commanded thee, saying: "Testify this testimony over Israel: see how it happened to the Shechemites and their sons, how they were given into the hands of the two sons of Jacob, and they slew them in torments, and it was justice to them, and it is written down for justice concerning them."

CHAP. XXXI. 1. And in the new moon of the month, Jacob spoke to all the men of his house, saying: "Purify yourselves and change your clothes, and arising let us go up to Bethel, where I made a vow when I was fleeing from the face of Esau, my brother; because he (God) has been with me, and has brought me into this land in peace. 2. And remove the false gods that are in your midst. 3. And tear away the false gods which are in your ears and on your necks, and the idols which Rachel took from her father Laban, and which she gave all to Jacob." 4. And he burned and broke and destroyed and hid them under an oak, which was in the land of Shechem. 5. And he ascended at the new moon of the seventh month to Bethel. 6. And he built an altar at the place where he had slept, and he erected there a monument, and he sent for his father Isaac to come to him to the sacrifice, and to his mother Rebecca. 7. And Isaac said: "Let my son Jacob come and let me see him before I die." 8. And Jacob went to Isaac his father, and to his mother Rebecca, to the house of his father Abraham, and he took two of his sons with him, Levi and Judah, and came to his father Isaac and his mother Rebecca. 9. And Rebecca came out of the tower to the front of the tower, that she might kiss Jacob and to embrace him, for her spirit was alive when she heard,

"Behold thy son Jacob has come!" and she kissed him. 10. And she saw the two sons and she knew them, and said to him: 11. "Are these thy sons, my son? " and she embraced them and kissed them and blessed them, saying: "In you may the seed of Abraham be honored, and may ye be a blessing over the earth!" 12. And Jacob went in to his father Isaac to his chamber where he slept, and his two sons with him, and he took the hand of his father, and bending down kissed him, and Isaac clung to the neck of Jacob his son, and wept on his neck. 13. And the darkness left the eyes of Isaac, and he saw the two sons of Jacob, Levi and Judah, and he said, "Are these thy sons, my Son? for they are like thee." 14. And he said that in truth they were his sons, and "in truth thou seest that they are my sons." 15. And they approached him, and they turned, and he kissed them and embraced them all together. 16. And the spirit of prophecy fell into his mouth, and he took Levi by the right hand, and Judah by the left hand. 17. And he turned to Levi and began to bless him first, saying, "May the Lord God of all, the Lord of all the worlds, bless thee and thy children in all the worlds. 18. And may the Lord give thee and thy seed greatness and great honor, and cause thee and thy seed to approach to him from among all flesh, that they shall serve him in his sanctuary like the angels of the face, and like the holy ones that shall be the seed of thy sons for honor and greatness and holiness: and may he make them great in all the worlds. 19. And they shall be princes and lords and leaders for all the seed of the sons of Jacob: they shall speak the words of the Lord in truth, and shall judge all his judgments in truth, and speak my ways to Jacob, and they shall appear to Israel: may the blessing of the Lord be given into their mouths, that they may bless all the seed of the beloved. 20. And thy mother has called thy name Levi, and in truth has she thus called thee: thou shalt be very near to the Lord, and shalt have a part with all the sons of Jacob: his table shall be thine, and thou and thy sons shall eat thereof, and to all the generations may thy table be full, and may thy food, not decrease to all eternity. 21. And all those that hate thee shall fall before thee, and all thy enemies shall be rooted out and be destroyed, but they that bless thee shall be blessed, and all the nations that curse thee shall be cursed." 22. And to Judah he spoke: "May the Lord give thee strength and power that thou mayest tread down all that hate thee: be thou a prince, thou and one of thy sons over the sons of Jacob. 23. May thy name and the name of thy sons be one that goes and encompasses the whole earth and the cities; then shall the Gentiles fear thy face, and all the nations shall tremble and all the people shake. 24. In thee let there be help to Jacob, and in thee may deliverance be found for Israel. 25. And if thou sittest on the throne of the honor of thy righteousness, there shall be great peace to all the seed of the sons of the beloved. 26. He that blesseth thee shall be blessed, and all that hate and trouble thee, and those that curse thee, shall be rooted out and be destroyed from the earth, and shall be accursed." 27. And turning around he kissed him again and embraced him and rejoiced greatly; for he had seen sons of Jacob, who was his son in truth. 28. And he came from between his feet, and fell down and prostrated himself, and he blessed them, and he remained with Isaac, his father, on that night, and they ate and drank with joy. 29. And he caused the two sons of Jacob to sleep, the one at his right, and other at his left, and it was accounted to him for righteousness. 30. And Jacob told his father everything during the night, how the Lord had been merciful to him, and how he had prospered him in all his ways and had protected him from all evil. 31. And Isaac blessed the God of his father Abraham, who had not ceased his mercy and righteousness from the sons of his servant Isaac. 32. And in the morning Jacob told his father Isaac of the vow he had made to the Lord, and of the vision he had seen, and how he had built an altar, and that everything was ready for the sacrifice before the Lord, as he had vowed, and that he had come to place him upon an ass. 33. And Isaac said to his sons Jacob: "I am not able to go with thee, for I am old and not able to endure the way: go, my son, in peace, for I am one hundred and sixty-five years old to-day; I am not able to travel. 34. Take thy mother and let her go with thee. 35. And I know, my son, that thou hast come on my account; and may this day be blessed upon which thou hast seen me alive and I have seen thee, my son. 36. Prosper, and fulfil the vow which thou hast vowed, and do not delay thy vow, for thou must seek the vow. 37. And now hasten to fulfil thy vow; and may he be pleased who has made all things, to whom thou hast made thy vow." 38. And he said to Rebecca: "Go with Jacob, thy son." 39. And Rebecca went with Jacob, and Deborah with her, and they came to Bethel. 40. And Jacob remembered the prayer with which his father had blessed him and his two sons, Levi and Judah, and he rejoiced and blessed the God of his fathers, Abraham and Isaac. 41. And he said: "Now I know that I have an eternal hope, and my sons also before the God of all; and thus it is ordained concerning the two, and they have placed it as a testimony for them to eternity, upon the tablets of heaven as Isaac blessed them.

CHAP. XXXII. 1. And he remained in that night in Bethel, and Levi dreamed that they had appointed and made him priest, and his sons to eternity, priests of the Most High God; and he awoke from his sleep and blessed the Lord. 2. And Jacob started early in the morning, on the fourteenth of this month, and the tenth of all that came with him of men and beasts, and gold, and all possessions and clothing. 3. And in those days Rachel became pregnant with her son Benjamin, and Jacob counted his sons from him on and upwards; and the portion of the Lord fell upon Levi, and his father clothed him with the garments of the priesthood, and filled his hands. 4. And on the fifteenth of this month he brought to the altar fifteen oxen from among the cattle, twenty-eight rams, and forty-nine sheep, and sixty lambs, and twenty-nine young goats, as a burnt sacrifice on the altar, and as an acceptable gift for a sweet savor to the Lord God.   5. This was the fulfilment of the vow he had made to give the tenth; together with their fruit and their drink offerings.   6. And when the fire had consumed them, he scattered frankicense over them on the fire; and for thank offering two oxen, and four rams, and four sheep, and a sheep of two years, and two young goats; thus he did distributing over seven days.   7. And he remained there eating, and all his sons and his men in joy seven days, and he blessed and thanked the Lord, who had delivered him from all his trouble, and to whom he had fulfilled his vow.   8. And he took the tenth of all the clean animals and made a burnt offering; and the unclean animals he gave to his son, and the men he gave him, and Levi exercised his priestly office in Bethel before Jacob, his father, in preference to his ten brothers, and he was there a priest, and Jacob fulfilled to him his vows: and thus he gave the tenth again to the Lord, and sanctified it, and it was holy for him. 9. And on this account it is ordained on the tablets of heaven as a law concerning the giving of a second tenth — to eat before the Lord at the place upon which he has chosen his name to dwell year after year, and to this law there is no limit of day to eternity.   10. And this ordinance is written to do it year after year for eating a second tenth before the Lord in the place which he has chosen, and nothing shall be left over from it to the following year.   11. For in its year shall the seed be eaten until the seed of the year and the wine change their days to the days of wine and oil, and to the days of oil in its season.   12. And all that is left thereof and which becomes old, let it be considered contaminated; burn it with fire, for it is unclean.   13. And thus they shall eat together in the sanctuary, and shall not let it become old.   14. And all the tenth of oxen and sheep shall be holy to the Lord, and shall belong to his priests, who will eat it before him from year to year; for thus it is ordained and engraven concerning the tenth on the tablets of heaven.   15. And in the following night, on the twenty-second day of this month, Jacob planned that he would build this place and erect a wall around it, and that he would sanctify it and make it holy to eternity, for himself and his children after him.   16. And the Lord appeared to him in the night, and blessed him, and said to him: "Thou shalt not call thy name Jacob only, but Israel also shall thy name be called."   17. And he said to him again: "I am the Lord thy God, who has created heaven and earth; and I will increase and multiply thee exceedingly, and kings shall come from thee, and they shall rule over all, wherever the foot of the sons of man has trod.   18. And I will give to thy seed all the land under heaven, and they shall rule over all the nations as they desire, and after that they will gather to themselves the whole earth, and shall inherit the world."   19. And he completed conversing with him, and ascended from there, and Jacob looked until he ascended to heaven. 20. And he saw in a vision of the night, and behold an angel descended from heaven with seven tablets in his hands, and he gave them to Jacob, and he read all that was written on them, what would happen to himself and his sons in all the years. 21. And he showed him all things that were written on the tablets, and said to him: "Do not build up this place, and do not make it an eternal sanctuary, and do not dwell here, for this is not the place. 22. Go to the house of Abraham, thy father, and dwell there with Isaac, thy father, until the day of the death of thy father. 23. For in Egypt thou shalt die in peace, and in this land thou shalt be buried in honor, in the grave of thy fathers, with Abraham and Isaac. 24. Fear not; for as thou hast seen and read it, thus shall it all be. 25. But write thou down all as thou hast seen and read." 26. And Jacob said: "How can I remember all as I have seen and read it?" 27. And he said to him: "I will recall it all for thee." 28. And he went up from there: and he awoke from his sleep and remembered all that he had seen and read, and he wrote down all the words that he had read and that he had seen. 29. And he stayed there yet another day, and sacrificed there according to all that had been ordained on former days, and called its name "addition," for this day was added; and the first day he called "the festival." 30. And thus it appeared that it would be, and it is written on the tablets of heaven; and on this account it was revealed to him, that he should celebrate it, and that he should add it to the seven days of the festival, and its name was called "addition," because it comes to the seven days; and thus is the festival by number of days of the year. 31. And in the night of the twenty-third of this month, Deborah, the nurse of Rebecca, died, and he buried her below the city under the oak of the river, and called the name of this river "the river of Deborah," and of the oak, "lamentation oak of Deborah." 32. And Rebecca went and returned to her house, to Isaac, that she should prepare for his father a meal, as he loved it. 33. And he too went after his mother until he came to the land of Kebratan, and he dwelt there. 34. And Rachel in that night gave birth to a son, and called his name "Son of my sorrow," for she suffered in giving birth; but his father called him Benjamin, on the eleventh of the eighth month, in the first year of the sixth week of this jubilee. 35. And Rachel died there, and was buried in the land of Ephrathah, that is, Bethlehem; and Jacob erected upon the grave of Rachel a column, on the road above her grave.

CHAP. XXXIII. 1. And Jacob went and dwelt toward the north at Magdelraep. 2. And he went to his father Isaac, he and Leah, his wife, on the new moon of the tenth month. 3. And Reuben saw Balla, the maid of Rachel, the concubine of his father, while she was bathing in water at a hidden place, and he loved her. 4. And he hid himself at night, and he entered the house of Balla at night, and found her lying alone on her bed, and sleeping, and he lay down with her. 5. And she awoke, and saw, and behold, Reuben was lying with her on the bed; and she uncovered the edge and seized him and cried out, and discovered that it was Reuben, and she was ashamed on his account, and let go her hand from him, and he fled. 6. And she lamented on account of this thing exceedingly, and did not mention it to anybody. 7. And when Jacob returned and sought her, she said to him: "I am not clean for thee, for I have been defiled for thee, for Reuben has defiled me and lay with me in the night, and I was asleep and did not discover it until he uncovered the edge, and he lay with me." 8. And Jacob was very angry at Reuben that he had lain with Balla, for he had uncovered the covering of his father; and Jacob did not approach her any more, because Reuben had defiled her, for his deed was very wicked, for it is accursed before the Lord. 9. On this account it is written and ordained on the tablets of heaven, that a man shall not sleep with the wife of his father, and that he shall not uncover the covering of his father, for this is unclean; they must surely die together, the man that lies with the wife of his father, and the woman, for they do an unclean thing in the land. 10. And there shall be nothing unclean before our God in the nation he has chosen for himself as a kingdom. 11. And again it is written: "Cursed be the one that lieth with the wife of his father, for he hath uncovered the shame of his father, and all the holy ones of the Lord shall say: 'Thus be it! Thus be it!'" 12. And thou, Moses, command the children of Israel that they observe this word, for the punishment is death, and it is unclean, and there is no forgiveness to atone for a man that does this wicked deed, except slaying and stoning him to death, or rooting him out from amongst the people of our God. 13. For there shall not remain alive on earth a single day any man that does this in Israel, for it is accursed and unclean. 14. And let them not say that Reuben lived and was forgiven that he had slept with the concubine of his father, and she too, although her husband, Jacob, his father, was yet alive. 15. For he had not yet revealed the ordinance and the punishment and the law in its entire completeness; for in thy days it is as a law since his days and as a law to eternity, to the generation of eternity; and there is not any passing of days to this law, nor any forgiveness to him, except that they both be rooted out together from the midst of the people: on the day on which they do it they shall slay them. 16. And thou, Moses, write it down for Israel that they observe it according to these words, and let them not commit a mortal sin, for the Lord our God is a judge who has no regard for persons and receives no presents. 17. And tell them these words of ordinance, that they obey and preserve them, and watch themselves, and be not destroyed and rooted out of the land; for unclean and an abomination and contamination and profanation are all they that do this on the earth before our God. 18. And there is no sin on earth greater than fornication, which they commit on the earth, for Israel is a nation holy unto God, and a nation of inheritance for its God, and a nation of priesthood and royalty and a possession, and no one shall appear thus unclean in the midst of the holy people. 19. And in the third year of this sixth week Jacob and all his sons went and dwelt in the house of Abraham, near Isaac, his father, and Rebecca, his mother. 20. And these are the names of the sons of Jacob: the first bore Reuben, Simeon, Levi, Judah, Issachar, Zebulun, the sons of Leah; and the sons of Rachel, Joseph and Benjamin; and the sons of Balla, Dan and Naphtali; and the sons of Zalapha, Gad and Asur; and Dinah, the daughter of Leah, the only daughter of Jacob. 21. And going, they bowed down before Isaac and Rebecca; and when they saw them, they blessed Jacob and all his sons. 22. And Isaac rejoiced exceedingly that he saw all the sons of Jacob, his youngest son, and he blessed them.

CHAP. XXXIV. 1. And in the sixth year of this week of the forty-fourth jubilee, Jacob sent his sons to pasture his sheep, and his servants with them to the pasture of Shechem. 2. And the seven kings of the Amorites assembled themselves against them to slay them, hiding themselves under the trees, and to take away their cattle and their wives. 3. And Jacob and Levi and Judah and Joseph were at the house where Isaac their father was, for his spirit was sad, and they could not leave him; and Benjamin was the youngest, and on this account remained with his father. 4. And the kings of Tapho and of Azesa and Saragon and Selo and Gaez, and the king of Betoron and of Manisaker came, and all those that dwell in those mountains, who dwell in the woods of the land of Canaan. 5. And they announced this to Jacob, saying: "Behold the kings of the Amorites have surrounded thy sons in order to rob their herds." 6. And he arose from his house, he and his three sons and the young men of his father, and went forth and went against them, eight hundred men who carried swords. 7. And they slew them on the fields of Shechem, and pursued those that fled and slew them with the edge of the sword, and slew them at Aresa and Thapha and Seragen and Selo and Amanisakero and Gagaas. 8. And he collected his herds; and he was more powerful than those and ordained a tax over them, that they should give him tribute, fine fruits of their land, and he built Reuben and Tamnatares. 9. And he returned in peace, and made peace with them, and they were his servants until the day he and his sons descended down to the land of Egypt. 10. And in the seventh year of this week he sent Joseph to learn about the safety of his brothers, from his house to Shechem, and he found them in the land of Dothan. 11. And they waylaid him and made a plot against him to slay him; and changing, they sold him to Ishmaelite merchants, and they brought him to Egypt, and sold him to Potiphar, the eunuch of Pharoah, the head cook, the one that sacrificed in the city of Elew.

12. And the sons of Jacob killed a young goat, and dipped the clothes of Joseph in its blood, and sent it to their father Jacob.   13. And it was on the tenth of the seventh month, and they stayed all this day until the evening, and they brought it to him; and he became fevered in his grief unto death, and said: "A wild beast has devoured Joseph;" and on that day all the men of his house were with him, and mourned and lamented with him all the day.   14. And his sons and his daughter arose to comfort him, but he could not be comforted on account of his son.   15. And on that day Balla heard that Joseph had been killed, and she died in her grief, and she was living at Kertaretef; and Dinah, his daughter, died also after Joseph had been slain.   16. This threefold sorrow came over Israel in one month.   17. And he buried Balla opposite the grave of Rachel, and Dinah, his daughter, he also buried there.   18. And he continued mourning for Joseph one year, and did not cease, saying: "I will descend into the grave grieving for my son."   19. And on this account it is ordained for the children of Israel, that they shall mourn on the tenth of the seventh month, on the day when they brought the sad news concerning Joseph to his father Jacob, that on it pardon should be sought by the death of a young goat, on the tenth of the seventh month, once a year, for their sins; for they had grieved the heart of their father on account of his son Joseph.   20. And this day has been ordained that they shall lament on it over their sins, and on account of all their transgressions, and on account of their error, that they shall cleanse themselves on this day once a year.   21. And after the death of Joseph the sons of Jacob took wives to themselves: first, the name of the wife of Reuben is Ada; secondly, the name of the wife of Simeon is Adiba, a Canaanite woman; third, the name of the wife of Levi is Melka, from among the daughters of Aram, from the seed of the sons of Taram; fourth, the name of the wife of Judah is Betasuel, a Canaanite woman; fifth, the name of the wife of Issachar is Jesakor Hezka; sixth, the name of the wife of Zebulun is Niiman; seventh, the name of the wife of Dan, Egla; eighth, the name of the wife of Naphtali is Rasua, of Mesopotamia; ninth, the name of the wife of Gad is Mak; and tenth, name of the wife of Asur is Ijon; eleventh, the name of the wife of Joseph is Asneth, an Egyptian woman; twelfth, the name of the wife of Benjamin is Ijoska.   22. And Simeon repented and took a second wife from Mesopotamia, like his brothers.

CHAP. XXXV.   1. And in the first year of the first week of the forty-fifth jubilee, Rebecca called her son Jacob and gave him command concerning his father and concerning his brother, that he should honor them all the days of the life of Jacob.   2. And Jacob said: "I will do all thou commandest me, for this thing will be honor and greatness to me and righteousness before the Lord, that I should honor them.   3. And thou, my mother, knowest me from the time I was born until this day, all my deeds and everything that is in my heart, that always I think good concerning all. 4. And how should I not do this which thou hast commanded me, that I should honor my father and my brother? 5. Tell me, my mother, what perversity thou seest in me? 6. And I am far removed from him, and gentleness is in me." 7. And she said to him: "My son, all my days I have not seen in thee any perversity, and no depraved actions, but righteousness. 8. But in truth I tell thee, my son, I will die in this year, and will not get beyond this year in my life, for I saw in a dream the day of my death, that I should not live beyond one hundred and fifty-five years. 9. And behold, I have completed all the days of my life which I was to live." 10. And Jacob laughed at the words of his mother, because she said that she would die, and she was sitting opposite him with her strength upon her, without any decrease of strength, for she went in and out, and saw, and her teeth were strong, and no ailment had touched her all the days of her life. 11. And Jacob said to her: "Happy am I, my mother, if my days approach the days of thy life, and my strength abide in me as thy strength; and thou wilt not die, for in vain dost thou speak with me concerning thy death." 12. And she went in to Isaac, and said to him: "One petition I ask of thee: let Esau swear that he will not harm Jacob, and will not persecute him in enmity, for thou knowest the thoughts of Esau, that he was terrible from his youth on, and there is not gentelness in him; for he desires after thy death to kill him. 13. And thou knowest how he has done all the days from the day when Jacob, his brother, went to Haran to this day, that he has left us with his whole heart, and does evil with us. 14. He has collected thy flocks, and all thy possessions he robs from before thy face, and when we entreated and asked for what was ours, he did as a man that practices usury on us. 15. And he is bitter at thee because thou didst bless that perfect and righteous son Jacob; for in him there is no evil, but goodness. 16. And since he came from Haran to this day, he has not deprived us of the least; but he brings us everything in its time and always, and he rejoices in his whole heart when we take anything from his hands, and he blesses us and does not separate from us since he came from Haran to the present day, and he lives with us ever in our house, honoring us." 17. And Isaac said to her: "I know and I see the deeds of Jacob with us, that with all his heart he honors us; but I loved Esau formerly more than Jacob, on acocunt of his birth; but now I love Jacob more than Esau, because he has increased in evil doings, and there is no righteousness in him, for all his ways are injustice and violence, and there is no righteousness in him at all. 18. And now my heart trembles concerning all his deeds, and neither he nor his seed shall abide, for they shall be destroyed from the earth, and they shall be rooted out from under heaven; for he has deserted the God of Abraham, and goes after his women after uncleanness and after error, he and his children. 19. And thou dost tell me that I shall make him swear not to kill Jacob:

even if he swears he will not keep to his oath, and will not do good but evil. 20. And if he desires to kill his brother Jacob, he shall be given into the hands of Jacob and shall not escape from his hands, but fall into his hands. 21. And thou fear not concerning Jacob, for the watchman of Jacob is great and powerful, and honored and worshipped above the watchman of Esau." 22. And Rebecca sent for and called Esau, and he came to her, and she said to him, "One prayer I have, my son, which I ask of thee, and grant it, that thou mayest do what I ask of thee, my son." 23. And he said to her: "I will do all that thou tellest me, and will not refuse any thing that thou askest." 24. And she said to him: "I ask of thee that the day I die thou wilt take me and bury me near the grave of Sarah, the mother of thy father, and that thou and thy brother Jacob will love each other, and that neither will undertake evil against his brother, but love him, so that ye may be prosperous, my son, and be honored in the midst of the land and that an enemy may not rejoice over you, and that ye may be a blessing and mercy before the eyes of all that love you." 25. And he said: "I will do all that thou sayest to me, and I will bury thee on the day of thy death near Sarah, the mother of thy father, as thou lovest her bones, that they shall be near to thy bones. 26. But Jacob, my brother, I will love above all flesh, and I have no other brother in all the world except him alone, and this is not a great thing for me that I shall love him, for he is my brother, and together we were sown in thy womb, and together we came forth from thee, and if I do not love my brother, whom shall I love? 27. And I then beg of thee that thou wilt exhort Jacob concerning me and concerning my children, for I know that he will rule as king over me and over my children, for on the day when my father blessed him, he made him the higher and me the lower. 28. And I swear to thee that I will love him and will not seek out evil against him all the days of my life, but only good." 29. And he swore to her concerning this whole matter. 30. And she called Jacob before the eyes of Esau, and commanded him according to the words she had spoken with Esau. 31. And he said, "I will do thy pleasure, promising that no evil shall proceed from me and from my sons against Esau, my brother, and nothing shall be shown him except love." 32. And they ate and drank, she and her sons, on this day, and she died, three jubilees and one week and one year old, in this night, and her two sons, Esau and Jacob, buried her in the cave near Sarah, the mother of their father.

CHAP. XXXVI. 1. In the sixth week of this year, Isaac called his two sons, Esau and Jacob, and they came to him, and he said to them: "My sons, I shall go the way of my father into the house of eternity, where my fathers are. 2. Bury me near to Abraham, my father, in the south cave in the field of Ephron, the Hittite, which Abraham bought as a burial place; there bury me. 3. And this I command you, my sons, that ye practise righteousness and rectitude on the earth, so that the Lord may bring upon you all that the Lord said that he would do to Abraham and to his seed. 4. And be ye to each other as loving brothers as a man that loves himself, and each seeking for his brother that which is good for him, and acting together from the heart upon earth, and loving each other as yourselves. 5. And concerning the matter of idols, I command ye, that ye cast them away and hold them in abomination, and hate them, and that ye do not love them, for they are full of deception for those that worship them, and for those that bow down to them. 6. And remember, O my sons, the Lord God of Abraham, your father, and how I too worshipped him and served him in truth, that he may increase you in joy and may enlarge your seed like the stars of the heaven in multitude, and plant you upon the earth as a plant of righteousness, which is not rooted out to all the generations of eternity. 7. And now I will make you swear a great oath, for there is no oath greater than the one by the glorious and honored and great name of him who created the heavens and the earth and all things together, that ye will fear and worship him, and that each will love his brother in tenderness and in truth, and that neither will wish evil against his brother, from now on to eternity, all the days of your life, that ye may be prosperous in all your deeds, and be not destroyed. 8. And if either of you devises evil against his brother, know from now on, that every one that devises evil against his brother shall fall into his hands, and shall be rooted out of the land of the living, and his seed shall be destroyed from under heaven. 9. And on that day of cursing and turbulence he (God) will also burn with devouring fire, as he burned Sodom, thus also will he burn his land and his city and all that is his, and he will be erased out of the book of the discipline of the sons of men, and shall not ascend into the book of life, for he shall be destroyed and shall depart to the eternal curse, so that for all days their punishments may be renewed in hate and in cursing, and in wrath, and in torments, and in fury, and in plagues, and in sickness to eternity. 10. And I say and testify to you, my sons, how that my judgment will come upon the man who desires to do evil against his brother." 11. And he divided all the possessions he had between the two on that day, and he gave the preference to him that was born first, both the tower and all around it, and everything that Abraham possessed around the well of the oath. 12. And he said: "This preference shall be his who was born first." 13. And Esau said: "I have sold and given my age to Jacob, to him it has been given, and I will not say anything more about it, not one word, for it is passed." 14. And Isaac said: "May blessing rest upon you, my sons, and upon your seed this day, for ye have given me rest, and my heart is not sad on account of the birthright, that no strife will take place concerning it. 15. The Most High Lord bless the man that does righteousness, him and his seed to eternity." 16. And he ended commanding them and blessing them, and they ate and drank before him together; and he rejoiced, for there was a reconciliation between them, and they went out from him and rested on that day and slept. 17. And Isaac slept on his bed that day rejoicing, and he slept the sleep of eternity, and died one hundred and eighty years old. 18. And he completed twenty-five weeks and five years. 20. And Esau went to the land of Edom, to the mountains of Seir and dwelt there. 21. And Jacob dwelt in the land of Hebron, in the tower of the land of the pilgrimage of his father Abraham, and worshipped God with his whole heart, and according to the command of him who appeared to him, who had distinguished him on the day of his birth. 22. And Leah, his wife, died, in the fourth year of the second week of the forty-fifth jubilee, and he buried her in the double cave near to Rebecca, his mother, to the left of the grave of Sarah, the mother of his father. 23. And all of her sons and his sons came to weep over Leah, his wife, with him, and that they might comfort each other on her account, for he mourned over her. 24. For he loved her exceedingly after Rachel her sister died, for she was perfect and righteous in all her ways and honored Jacob: and in all the days which she lived she was gentle and upright and peaceful and honorable. 25. And he remembered all her deeds which she had done in her life, and mourned exceedingly, for he loved her very much with all his heart and with all his soul.

CHAP. XXXVII. 1. And on the day of the death of Isaac, the father of Jacob and Esau, when the sons of Esau heard that Isaac had given the birthright to his younger son Jacob, they were very angry. 2. And they quarrelled with their father, saying: "Why hath thy father, although thou art the elder and Jacob the younger, given to Jacob the birthright and left thee behind?" 3. And he said to them: "Because I sold my right of first birth to Jacob for a small mess of lentils. 4. And on the day that my father sent me to hunt and catch and bring something to him that he should eat it and bless me, he came in deception and brought to my father something to eat and to drink, and my father blessed him and put me under his hand. 5. And now our father has made us swear, me and him, that we will not devise any evil one against his brother, and that each will continue in love and in peace with his brother, and will not destroy our ways." 6. And they said to him: "We will not listen to thee to keep peace with him, for our strength exceeds his strength, and we are more powerful than he. 7. We will go out against him, and will slay him, and destroy his children; and if thou dost not go with us, we will do thee harm also. 8. Listen now to us: We will send to Aram and to Philistia and to Moab and to Ammon, and we will pick out for ourselves chosen men who are prepared for battle, and we will go against him and will battle with him, and we will root him out of the land, before he has taken root and is strong." 9. And their father said to them: "Ye shall not go and make war upon him, that ye may not fall before him." 10. And they said to him: "This is as thou hast done from thy youth on to the present day, and thou hast brought thy neck under his yoke. 11. We will not listen to these words." And they sent to Aram and to Aduram to the associates of their father, and they hired with themselves one thousand fighting men and chosen warriors. 12. And there came to them from Moab and from the children of Ammon those that were hired, one thousand chosen men, and from Philistia one thousand chosen warriors, and from Edom and the Horites one thousand chosen fighters, and from the Hittites strong fighting men. 13. And they said to their father: "Go out, lead them, and if not, we will kill thee." 14. And he was filled with anger and wrath at the time when he saw his sons that they were forcing him to go before them to lead them against Jacob, his brother. 15. And then he remembered all the evil which had been hidden in his heart against his brother Jacob, and did not remember the oath which he had sworn to his father and his mother, that he would not devise any evil all his days against his brother Jacob. 16. And in all this time Jacob did not know that they were coming against him for battle, but he was lamenting over Leah, his wife, until they approached him very near to the tower, four thousand warlike, powerful, and chosen fighters. 17. And the men of Hebron sent to him saying: "Behold thy brother is coming against thee to fight with thee with four thousand heavily girded men, and they carry shields and weapons;" for they loved Jacob more than Esau, and told it to him, for Jacob was a more gracious and mild man than Esau. 18. But Jacob did not believe it until he approached very near the tower. 19. And he fastened the gates of the tower and stood upon the top of the tower, and spoke with his brother Esau and said: "Hast thou come to me bringing me a good consolation on account of my wife who has died? 20. Is this the oath which thou hast sworn to thy father and thy mother twice before they died? 21. Thou hast violated the oath, and on account of what thou hast sworn to thy father, thou shalt be judged." 22. And then Esau answered and said to him: "There is not to the sons of men and to the animals of the earth any oath of trust which they swear to them unto eternity; but on that morning yet they devise evil against each other, so that one may kill his hater and his enemy. 23. And thou too dost hate me and my children to eternity, and there is no brotherly dealing with thee. 24. Hear these my words which I announce to thee: If one can change the bristles of the swine and change them into wool, and if horns will come out of its head like the horns of the deer and rams, then I will maintain brotherly relations with thee. 25. And if the breasts are separated from the mother — for wast not thou to me a brother — and if the wolves make peace with the lambs, so that they do not devour and rob them; and if their hearts incline to doing each other good, then will there be peace in my heart toward thee. 26. And when the lion becomes the friend of the ox, and when he is put into one yoke with him and plows with him, then I will make peace with thee. 27.

And when the raven becomes white like the rice bird, then I will know that I love thee and will make peace with thee. Thou shalt be rooted out and thy sons shall be rooted out, and there shall be no peace." 28. And then Jacob saw that his heart was evil against him, and that from his whole soul he would slay him, and he had come springing like a wild animal which comes against the spear that pierces it through and kills it, and it does not depart from it. 29. And then he said to his sons and to his servants that they should attack him and all his companions.

CHAP. XXXVIII. 1. And after that Judah spoke to his father Jacob and said to him: "Bend thy bow, Father, and send forth thy arrows and cast down thy hater and slay thy enemy: and mayest thou have the power, for we will not slay thy brother, for to thee and with thee and to us it will be an honor." 2. And immediately Jacob bent the bow and sent forth his arrow, and cast down his brother Esau, and slew him. 3. And again he sent forth his arrow and hit Adoran, the Aramaean, on the left breast, and drove him back and killed him. 4. And then the sons of Jacob and their servants came out breaking forth from the four sides of the tower. 5. Out came completely Judah, and Naphtali and Gad with him, and fifty young men with him out of the north side of the tower, and killed all that they found before them, and non escaped of those, not one. 6. And Levi and Dan and Asher came out from the east side of the tower, and fifty with them, and they slew the warriors of Moab and Ammon. 7. And Reuben and Issachar and Zebulun came out of the south side of the tower, and fifty with them, and they killed the fighters or Philistia. 8. And Simeon and Benjamin and Enoch, the son of Reuben, came out of the west side of the tower, and fifty with them, and killed of those of Edom and Choran four hundred powerful men, and seven hundred escaped, and four of the sons of Esau fled with them, and left their father behind dead, as he had fallen on the hill which is (called) Aduram. 9. And the sons of Jacob pursued after them to the mountains of Seir, and made them bend their necks, so that they became the servants of the sons of Jacob; and they sent word to their father inquiring if they should make peace with them, or if they should kill them. 11. And Jacob sent word to his sons that they should make peace; and they made peace with them, and they placed the yoke of servitude upon them that they should pay tribute to Jacob and his sons all the days. 12. And they continued to pay tribute to Jacob until the day when Jacob descended to the land of Egypt, and the sons of Esau did not cease from the yoke of servitude which the twelve sons of Jacob had imposed upon them, until the present day. 13. And these are the kings which ruled over Edom before a king ruled over the children of Israel, until the present day in the land of Edom; and Balak, the son of Beor, was king, and the name of his city was Dinaba. 14. And Balak died, and Jobab, the son of Zara, of Bezor, ruled in his stead. 15.

And Jobab died, and Adat, the son of Barad, who slew the Mediarites on the field of Moab, was king in his place, and the name of his city was Amot. 16. And Adat died and Salman, of Amalek, was king in his stead. 17. And Salman died and Saul, of the river Robaet, was king in his stead. 18. And Saul died, and Beulunan, the son of Akbur, was king in his stead. 19. And Beulunan died, and Adat was king in his stead, and the name of his wife was Matilat, the daughter of Matrit, the daughter of Metbed Zaab. 20. These are the kings who ruled in the land of Edom.

CHAP. XXXIX. 1. And Jacob dwelt in the land of the pilgrimage of his father, the land of Canaan. 2. These are the generations of Jacob: When Joseph was seventeen years old they took him down into Egypt, and sold him to Potiphar, the eunuch of Pharoah, the head of the cooks. 3. And he set Joseph over his whole house: and the blessing of the Lord was in the house of the Egyptian on account of Joseph, and all that he did the Lord prospered. 4. And the Egyptian left in Joseph's hands all that was before him, for he saw that the Lord was with him, and that everything he did the Lord prospered. 5. But Joseph was beautiful to look at and very attractive in form, and the wife of the master lifted up her eyes and saw Joseph. 6. And she loved him and entreated him to lie with her. 7. But he did not give over his soul, but remembered the Lord and the words which his father Jacob had read from among the words of Abraham, that no one among men should commit fornication with the wife of another, and with a woman who has a husband, and that as a punishment for this one death has been established in the heavens before the Most High God, and the sin on account of it will be inscribed on the books which are in eternity, all the days, before the Lord. 8. And Joseph remembered these words, and was not willing to lie with her. 9. And she entreated him one year, and he refused, and would not listen. 10. But she embraced him and seized him in the house in order to force him to lie with her, and locked the doors of the house; but he tore himself out of her hands and left his garment in her hand, and broke the lock, and fled without away from her presence. 11. And the woman saw that he would not lie with her, and shed lied before her lord, saying: "Thy Hebrew servant, whom thou lovest, sought to do me violence that he might lie with me, and it happened that when I raised my voice, he fled and left his garment in my hand, when I had seized him, and broke the lock." 12. And the Egyptian saw the garment of Joseph and the broken lock, and he obeyed the words of his wife, and cast Joseph into prison, into the place where the prisoners stayed whom the king had caused to be imprisoned. 13. And there he was in prison, and the Lord gave Joseph grace in the eyes of the head of the prison guards, and good will before him, for he saw that the Lord was with him, and all that he did the Lord prospered. 14. And he left all things to him, and the head of the prison guards looked to nothing, for all things that Joseph did the Lord perfected.   15. And he remained there two years.   16. And in those days Pharoah was angry with two of his eunuchs, the chief of the butlers and the chief of the bakers, and he cast them into prison, into the house of the chief of the cooks, the prison where Joseph was held.   17. And the chief of the prison guards ordered Joseph to serve them, and he served them before him.   18. And both of them dreamed a dream, the chief of the butlers and the chief of the bakers, and they told it to Joseph.   19. And as he explained to them, thus it happened to them; and the chief of the butlers Pharoah put back into his office, and the chief of the bakers he killed, as Joseph had explained to them.   20. And the chief of the butlers forgot Joseph in the prison, although he had informed him what would become of him, and did not remember to inform Pharoah as Joseph had told him, for he forgot.

CHAP. XL.   1. And in those days Pharoah dreamed two dreams in one night, concerning the matter of a famine which would come over all the land; and he awoke from his dream, and called all the dream interpreters that were in Egypt, and the sorcerers, and told them both his dreams, and they were not able to understand them. 2. And then the chief of the butlers recalled Joseph to memory, and spoke concerning him to the king; and he brought him out of prison and narrated his two dreams before him.   3. And he spoke before Pharoah that his two dreams were one, and he said: "Seven years will come of plenty over all the land of Egypt, and after that, seven years of famine, such as had not been upon the whole earth.   4. And now, O Pharoah, establish throughout the land of Egypt storehouses that grain may be gathered into them from city to city, in the days of the years of plenty, so that there may be grain for the seven years of famine, and that the land be not destroyed on account of the famine, for it will be very severe."   5. And the Lord gave Joseph grace and good will before the eyes of Pharoah, and Pharoah said to his servants: "We shall not be able to find a wise and intelligent man like this man, for the spirit of the Lord is upon him."   6. And he appointed him the second over the whole kingdom, and made him prince over all Egypt; and caused him to ride upon the second chariot of Pharoah, and clothed him with Byssus garments, and put a golden chain around his neck, and proclaimed before him, saying: "El El wa abrir." And he put (a ring) upon his hand, and made him master of his whole house, and made him great, and said to him: "I will not be greater than thee except in regard to the thronedom."   7. And Joseph was lord in all the land of Egypt, and all the princes of Pharoah loved him, and all the servants and all those that did the offices of the king, for he walked in rectitude and without pride and haughtiness of heart, and did not regard persons nor take bribes, but in rectitude he judged over all the peoples of the land.   8. And the land of Egypt was governed peacefully before Pharoah on account of Joseph, for the

Lord was with him, and gave him grace and good will over all his race, before all who knew him and heard reports concerning him; and the kingdom of Pharoah was in a right condition, without any enemy or evil. 9. And the king called the name of Joseph, Sephnetiphanz, and gave the daughter of Potiphar as a wife to Joseph, the daughter of one that sacrifices at Heliopolis, the chief of the cooks. 10. And on the day that Joseph stood before Pharoah he was thirty years old, when he stood before the face of Pharoah. 11. And in that year Isaac died. 12. And it happened as Joseph had said concerning the explanation of the two dreams, and there were seven years of plenty, and the land of Egypt was full of fruit, for one measure eighteen measures. 13. And Joseph gathered food from city to city, until they were full of grain, until they were not able to count and measure it on account of multitude.

CHAP. XLI. 1. And in the forty-fifth jubilee, in the second week in the second year, Judah took a wife for Er, his first-born, from among the daughters of Aram, and her name was Tamar. 2. And he hated her and did not lie with her, because his mother was from among the daughters of Canaan, and he desired to take a wife to himself from the relatives of his mother, but his father Judah would not permit him. 3. And this his first-born was wicked, and the Lord slew him. 4. And Judah said to his son Onan: "Go in to the wife of thy brother, and make her thy wife and raise up seed for thy brother." 5. And Onan knew that the seed would not be his, but rather his brother's, and he went to the house of the wife of his brother, and poured the seed upon the ground, and was wicked before the eyes of the Lord, and he slew him. 6. And Judah said to Tamar, his daughter-in-law, "Abide in the house of thy father as a widow until my son Shelah has grown, and I will give thee to him for a wife." 7. And he grew up; but Bedsuel, the wife of Judah, would not permit her son Shelah to marry her. 8. And Bedsuel, the wife of Judah, died in the fifth year of this week. 9. And in the sixth year thereof Judah went up to shear his sheep at Timnath. 10. And she laid aside her widow's garments and clothed herself with a vail, and beautified herself, and sat down at the gate on the way to Timnath. 11. And when Judah came, he found her, and thought her a harlot, and said to her: "I will go in to thee." 12. And she said to him, "Come in," and he came in unto her. 13. And she said to him, "Give me my pay." 14. And he said to her, "I have nothing in my hand except my ring on my finger and my bracelet and my staff, which is in my hand." 15. And she said to him, "Give me these until thou sendest me my pay." 16. And he said to her, "I will send thee a young kid;" and he gave them to her. 17. And she conceived from him; and Judah went to his sheep, but she went to the house of her father. 18. And Judah sent a young kid through a shepherd of Adullam, and he did not find her, and asked the people of the place, saying, "Where is the harlot which was here?" 19. And they said, "There has been no harlot here, and there is no harlot among us." 20. And he returned and told him that he had not found her, and said, "I asked the people of the place and they said to me that there was no harlot there." 21. And he said, "Arise, let us go that we do not become a laughing stock." 22. And when three months were over she learned that she was pregnant, and they told Judah, saying, "Behold, thy daughter-in-law Tamar has conceived by whoredom." 23. And Judah went to the house of her father, and said to her father and mother and brothers: "Bring her out that she be burned, for she has done an unclean thing in Israel. 24. And it happened when they brought her out to burn her, she sent to her father-in-law the ring and the bracelets and the staff, saying, "Dost thou recognize whose these are, for from him have I conceived?" 25. And Judah recognized them and said, "Tamar is more just than I." 26. And they did not burn her. 27. And on this account she was not given to Shelah; and he did not again approach her. 28. And after that she gave birth to two male children, Pharez and Zarah, in the seventh year of this second week. 29. And three more completed the seven years of fruitfulness of which Joseph had said to Pharoah. 30. And Judah knew that it was an evil deed which he had done, for he had lain with his daughter-in-law, and regarded it as a sin before his eyes, and he knew that he had sinned and erred, because he had uncovered the skirt of his son. 31. And he began to lament it and ask for mercy before the Lord on account of his sin. 32. And he told him in a dream, that it would be forgiven him, because he begged exceedingly for mercy and lamented, and did not repeat it. 33. And he obtained forgiveness, for he turned from his sin and ignorance, for it was a great transgression before the Lord our God; and every one that does thus, and lies with his daughter-in-law shall be burned with fire, that he may burn therein, for it is uncleanness and defilement upon them: with fire they shall be burnt. 34. And thou, Moses, command the children of Israel that there be no uncleanness among them, for every one that liety with his mother-in-law or his daughter-in-law does an unclean thing: with fire shall be burnt the man who lies with her, and the woman also, and he (God) shall remove the anger and punishment from Israel. 35. But to Judah he said that because his two sons did not lie with her, on that account his seed stands for a second generation, and should not be rooted out; for in innocence of his eyes he had gone and sought punishment, namely, according to the judgment of Abraham which he commanded his children, that Judah should be burned with fire.

CHAP. XLII. 1. And in the first year of the third week of the forty-fifth jubilee, the famine began to come into the land, and rain refused to be given to the earth; for none fell. 2. And the earth was unfruitful, and in the land of Egypt alone there was food, for Joseph had gathered that he might give them food, and Joseph had gathered seed of the earth in the seven years of fruitfulness and had guarded it.   3. And the Egyptians came to Joseph that he should give them food, and he opened the storehouses where the grain was in the first year, and he sold it to the people of the land for gold.   4. And Jacob heard that there was food in the land of Egypt, and he sent ten sons, that they should go for him to Egypt, but Benjamin he did not send. 5. And they came, together with those that went there.   6. And Joseph knew them, but they did not know him; and he spoke with and asked them, and said to them: "Are ye not spies and have come to examine the traces of the land?"   7. And he locked them in.   8. And then again he released them and incarcerated Simeon alone, and his nine brothers he sent away.   9. And he filled their sacks with grain, and he placed their gold in their sacks, and they did not know it. 10. And he commanded them that they should bring their youngest brother, for they had told him that their father was yet living and also their youngest brother.   11. And they went up from the land of Egypt, and came to the land of Canaan, and told their father all that had happened to them, and how the prince of the land had spoken with them and had seized Simeon until they should bring Benjamin. 12. And Jacob said, "Ye have robbed me of my children: Joseph is no more, Simeon is no more, and ye will also take Benjamin; your wickedness is upon you."   13. And he said: "My son shall not go with you; it is possible that he will become sick; for their mother has given birth to two sons, one is destroyed and this one ye will take.   14. He might take a fever on the road, and ye will bring my gray hairs in sorrow into death"   15. For he saw that all their gold was returned in their packages, and on this account he feared to send him.   16. But the famine increased and became strong in the land of Canaan, and in all the lands, except in the land of Egypt, for many of the sons of Egypt had gathered their seeds for food when they saw that Joseph was collecting the seed and placing it into the storehouses, and preserving it for the years of famine, and the men of Egypt fed themselves in the first year of their famine.   17. And when Israel saw that the famine was very powerful in the land, and that there was no deliverance, he said to his sons: "Go, return, and bring us food that we die not."   18. And they said: "We will not go: unless our youngest brother goes with us we will not go."   19. And Israel saw that if he would not send him with them all would be destroyed on account of the famine.   20. And Reuben said: "Give him to me into my hand, and if I do not return him to thee, slay my two sons in place of his soul."   21. And he said, "He shall not go with thee."   22. And Judah approached and said to him: "Send him with me; and if I do not bring him back to thee, I shall be a transgressor before thee all the days of my life."   23. And he sent him with them in the second year of this week in the new moon of the month, and they came into the land of Egypt with all those that went, and presents in their hands; and stacte and nuts and pistachio and pure honey.   24. And they came and stood before Joseph, and he saw his brother Benjamin, and knew him, and said to them: "Is this your youngest brother?" 25. And they said to him: "Yea, it is he." 26. And he said, "The Lord be merciful to thee, my son." 27. And he sent them into his house, and brought out Simeon to them and made them a feast, and they brought to him what they had brought in their hands. 28. And they ate before him, and he gave them all a portion of the others seven times, and they ate and drank, and arose and remained with their asses. 29. And Joseph thought out a plan how he could learn their thoughts, whether their thoughts were peace among each other; and he said to the man who was over his house: "Fill all their sacks with food, but their gold return to them in the midst of their receptacle, and my goblet out of which I drink put into the sack of the youngest, the silver goblet, and send them away."

CHAP. XLIII. 1. And he did as Joseph had told him, and filled all their sacks for them with food, but their gold he put into their sacks, and the goblet he put into the sack of Benjamin. 2. And early in the morning they departed. 3. And it happened when they had gone from there that Joseph said to the man: "Follow them, run and upbraid them, saying: 'For good ye have returned evil, and have stolen the silver cup out of which my master drinks.' And bring back to me their youngest brother, quickly before that I go to my official work." 4. And he ran after them and said to them according to these words. 5. And they said to him: "Far be it from thy servants to do this thing: we have not stolen out of the house of thy lord any utentil, and the gold which we found the first time in our sacks, we, thy servants, have brought back out of the land of Canaan. 6. How then would we steal any utensil: behold, here we are, and our sacks; search, and wherever thou findest the cup in the sack of any man among us, he shall be killed, but we and our asses will serve thy lord." 7. And he said to them: "Not thus, the man with whom I find it, him alone will I take as a servant, but ye shall return in peace to your houses. 8. And when he searched in their vessels, beginning with the oldest and ending with the youngest, it was found in the sack of Benjamin, the youngest. 9. And they were terrified and rent their clothes, and loaded their asses and returned to the city and came to the house of Joseph, and all fell down before him upon their faces on the ground. 10. And Joseph said to them: "Ye have done evil;" and they said to him: "What shall we say, and with what shall we defend ourselves that our Lord has found the guilt of his servants? 11. Behold, we are thy servants, O our lord, together with our asses." 12. And Joseph said to them: "I, too, fear the Lord, and ye shall go to your houses, but your youngest brother shall be my servant, for ye have done evil: do ye not know that one like me who drinks out of his cup values it? 13. And ye have stolen it." 14. And Judah said: "For us, my lord, let me speak a word into the ear of my lord: his mother has borne thy servant, our father, two sons; one has left and was lost, and no one found him, and this one alone is left from his mother; and thy servant, our father, loves him and his soul cleaves to his soul, and it will happen when we return to thy servant, our father, and if the young man is not with us, he will die, and our father will sink away through grief unto death. 15. But I will become a servant to my lord in the place of the boy; but let the youth go with his brothers, for I have given promise for him to thy servant, our father; and if thou dost not return him, then thy servant will be guilty to our father all the days." 16. And Joseph saw the heart of all that they were friendly to each other and well disposed, and he was not able to restrain himself, and he said that he was Joseph, and conversed with them in the Hebrew tongue, and he fell upon their neck and wept; but they had not known him, and began to weep. 17. And he said to them: "Do not weep over me; but hasten and bring my father to me, that I may see him before I die, and the eyes of my brother Benjamin while I see. 18. For, behold, this is the second year of the famine, and there are yet five years without any harvest or fruit of trees or any plants. 19. Hasten ye to come down with your households, so that ye be not destroyed by the famine, and do not grieve yourselves on account of yourselves, and on account of your possessions, for the Lord has sent me before you as a provider, that many people might live. 20. And tell my father that I am yet alive. 21. But ye, behold, see me, that the Lord has set me as a father to Pharoah, and that I should rule in his house and over all the land of Egypt. 22. And tell my father of all my honor and all the measure which the Lord has given me of wealth and of honor." 23. And at the command of Pharoah, he gave them wagons and provisions for the road and gave them all colored garments and silver and ten asses that carried grain and he sent them away. 25. And they went up and announced to their father that Joseph was alive, and that he was measuring out grain to all the nations of the earth, and that he was lord of all the land of Egypt. 26. And their father did not believe it, for he was terrified in his thoughts, but when he saw the wagons which Joseph had sent, his spirit revived and lived, and he said: "It is a great thing for me that Joseph lives: I will go down to see him before I die."

CHAP. XLIV. 1. And Israel arose from Haran, from his house, at the new moon of the third month, and came by the way of the well of the oath, and offered a sacrifice to the God of his father, Isaac, on the seventh of this month, and Jacob remembered the dream which he had dreamed at Bethel, and he feared to descend down to Egypt. 2. And while he was thinking that he would send word to Joseph that he should come to him, and the he would not go down, he remained there seven days, if he might see a vision, whether he should remain or go down. 3. And he celebrated the harvest festival of first fruits with old grain, for there was not a handful of seed in all the land of Canaan, for it was unfruitful for all the animals and beasts and birds, and also human beings.   4. And on the sixteenth thereof the Lord appeared to him and said to him: "Jacob, Jacob!"   5. And he said: "Here I am."   6. And he said to him: "I am the God of thy fathers Abraham and Isaac: fear not to go down to Egypt, for I will make thee into a great people.   7. I will go down with thee and I will bring thee back into this land that thou be buried here, and Joseph shall lay his hands upon thy eyes: fear not to go down to Egypt."   8. And he arose, and his sons and his sons' sons, and they placed their father and their vessels upon the wagons.   9. And Israel started from the well of the oath on the sixteenth of the third month, and went to the land of Egypt.   10. And Israel sent before him to Joseph, his son Judah, that he should examine the land of Goshen, for there Joseph had told his brothers that they should come, that they should dwell there, that they might be near him; and this was good in the land of Egypt and near to him, for them all and for their animals.   11. And these are the names of the sons of Jacob who went into Egypt with Jacob their father; Reuben, the first-born of Israel: and these are the names of his sons: Enoch and Phalus and Ezerom and Charami, five: Simeon and his sons, and these are the names of his sons: Ijamoel and Ijamen and Amet and Ijakim and Saar and Samel, the son of the Sephanite; seven: Levi and his sons; and these are the names of his sons, Gedson and Kaat and Merari, four: Judah and his sons; and these are the names of his sons: Selem and Phalus and Zara, four: Issachar and his sons; and these are the names of his sons: Tola and Phua and Ijaseb and Samarom, five: Zebulun and his sons, and these are the names of his sons: Azor and Elon and Ijaluel, four.   12. And these are the sons of Jacob and their sons whom Leah had borne to Jacob in Mesopotamia, six, and one sister to them, Dinah; and all the souls whom Leah had borne and their sons, who went with their father Jacob to Egypt, were twenty-nine, and Jacob, their father, with them, it thus was thirty.   13. And the sons of Zalapha, the handmaid of Leah, the wife of Jacob, whom she bore to Jacob: Gad and Asher. 14. And these are the names of their sons who went with them to Egypt; the sons of Gad: Zephjon and Agati and Somi and Asohen . . . and Aroli and Arodi; eight.   15. And the sons of Asher: Ijamua and Jesua and Barja and Sara, their sister, seven.   16. And all the souls are fourteen, and all of Leah were forty-four.   17. And the sons of Rachel, the wife of Jacob, were Joseph and Benjamin.   18. And to Joseph were born in Egypt before his father came to Egypt, whom Asnet bore him, the daughter of Potiphar, the sacrificer of Heliopolis, Manasseh and Ephraim, three.   19. The sons of Benjamin are Bala and Bachor and Esabel, Zuel and Neman and Abdlji and Rae and Sanaim and Aphem and Gaom, eleven.   20. And all the souls of Rachel were fourteen.   21. And the sons of Bila, the handmaid of Rachel, the wife of Jacob, were Dan and Naphtali.   22. And these are the names of their sons who went with them to Egypt; the sons of Dan are Chusi and Samon and Asudi and Ijak and Salamon, six.   23. And they died in Egypt in the year in which they went down, and there was left to Dan only Chusi. 24. And these are the names of the sons of Naphtali: Ijasiel and Guhani and Asaar and Suloni and Eme, six; and Eme died in Egypt, who was born after the year of the famine. 25. And all the souls of Rachel were twenty-six. 26. And all the souls of Jacob, that went with him to Egypt, were seventy souls; but his children and his children's children, all together were seventy-five, but five died in Egypt, who were not married and had no children; and in the land of Canaan two sons of Judah died, Er and Onan, and had no children. 27. And the sons of Israel buried those that were destroyed, and these were counted among the seventy peoples.

CHAP. XLV. 1. And Israel went to the land of Egypt unto the land of Goshen at the new moon of the fourth month of the second year of the third week of the forty-fifty jubilee. 2. And Joseph went to meet his father Jacob in the land of Goshen, and he fell upon the neck of his father and wept. 3. And Israel said to Joseph: "I would die now after I have seen thee. 4. And now may the Lord God of Abraham and Isaac be blessed, who has not withdrawn his mercy and kindness from his servant Jacob: It is a great thing to me that I have seen thy face in my life, for true is the vision which I saw in Bethel, blessed be the Lord God to all eternity, and blessed be his name." 5. And Joseph and his brothers ate bread before their father and drank wine; and Jacob rejoiced exceedingly much, for he saw that Joseph ate with his brothers and drank before him; and he blessed the Creator of all, who had preserved for him his twelve sons. 6. And Joseph gave his father and his brothers as a present that they should dwell in the land of Goshen and in Ramasitino, and their whole territory, that they should rule it before Pharoah. 7. And Israel and his sons dwelt in the land of Goshen, the best part of the land of Egypt: but Israel was one hundred and thirty years old when he came into Egypt. 8. And Joseph gave provisions to his father and brothers, and their possessions as much as supported them for the seven years of famine. 9. And the land of Egypt suffered on account of the famine, and Joseph gathered in all the land of Egypt to Pharoah for food, both the people and their cattle, and Pharoah possessed everything. 10. And the years of famine were completed, and Joseph gave to the people that were in the land of Egypt seed and food to sow in the eighth year, for the river had overflowed into all the land of Egypt. 11. For in the seven years of famine it had watered only a few spots along the bank of the river, but now it overflowed; and the Egyptians sowed upon their land and it produced much grain in that year. 12. And this was the first year of the fourth week of the thirty-fifty jubilee. 13. And Joseph took of the grain which they sowed the fifth part for the king, and the fourth he left them for food and for sowing: and Joseph made it a law for the land of Egypt unto this day. 14. And Israel lived in the land of Egypt seventeen years, and all the days which he lived were three jubilees, one hundred and forty-seven years.   15. And he died in the fourth year of the fifth week of the forty-fifth jubilee.   16. And Israel blessed his sons before he died, and told them everything as it would happen to them in the latter days, and everything he made known to them, and blessed them and gave Joseph two portions in the land.   17. And he slept with his fathers and was buried in the double cave in the land of Canaan beside Abraham, his father, in the grave which he had dug for himself, in the double cave, in the land of Hebron.   18. And he gave all his books and the books of his fathers to his son Levi, that he should guard them and renew them for the sons of Israel to this day.

CHAP. XLVI.   1. And it happened after the death of Jacob that the children of Israel increased in the land of Egypt.   2. And they became a great people, and they were all united in their hearts, so that each loved his brother and every man assisted his brother, and they increased and multiplied and increased very much.   3. And ten weeks of years were all the days of the life of Joseph which he lived after his father, and he was no enemy or anything wicked in all the days of the life of Joseph which he lived after his father Jacob, for all the Egyptians honored the sons of Jacob during all the days of the life of Joseph.   4. And Joseph died when he was one hundred and ten years old: seventeen years he lived in the land of Canaan and ten years he was a servant, and three years he was in prison, and eighty years he was under the king ruling all the land of Egypt.   5. And all his brothers died, and all that generation.   6. And he commanded the children of Israel, before he died, that they should carry up his bones when they would go out of the land of Egypt.   7. And he made them swear concerning his bones, for he knew that the Egyptians would not again bring out his bones and bury them in the land of Canaan, for Memkeron, the king of Canaan, while he was dwelling in the land of Asur, was fighting in the valley with the king of Egypt and killed him there and pursued the Egyptians to the gates of Eromon.   8. But he was unable to enter, for a second new king ruled over Egypt, and he was more powerful than he; and he returned to the land of Canaan, and the gates of Egypt were locked and no one entered Egypt.   9. And Joseph died in the forty-sixth jubilee, in the sixth week, in the second year; and they buried him in the land of Egypt, and all his brothers died after him.   10. And the king of Egypt went out to fight with the king of Canaan in the forty-seventh jubilee, in the second week, in the second year thereof; and the children of Israel brought out the bones of all the sons of Jacob except the bones of Joseph, and buried them in the fields, in the double caves in the mountains.   11. And the most returned to Egypt, and a few of them remained behind in the mountains of Hebron, and thy father Anbaram (Amram) remained with them.   12. And the king of Canaan overcame the king of Egypt and locked the portals of Egypt.   13. And he devised an evil plan against the children of Israel that he would torment them, and he said to the men of Egypt: "Behold, the people of the children have increased and multiplied more than we; behold, we will plot against them before they become too many, and will torment them with slavery, before a murder comes over us and before these become our enemies; if not, these will unite with the enemy and will depart out of our land, for their faces and hearts are toward the land of Canaan." 14. And he set over them work-overseers that they should torment them with slave work. 15. And they commanded them, and they built strong cities for Pharoah, Pithom and Ramese, and they built all the walls and sides which had fallen in in the cities of Egypt. 16. And they oppressed them with service, but as much as they abused them so much they increased and so much they multiplied. 17. And the men of Egypt considered the children of Israel unclean.

CHAP. XLVII. 1. And in the seventh week, in the seventh year, in the forty-seventh jubilee, thy father came from the land of Canaan, and thou wast born in the fourth week, in the sixth year, in the forty-eighth jubilee, which are the days of the persecution over the sons of Israel. 2. And King Pharoah, of Egypt, issued a command concerning them, that they should throw all their children, every make, into the river. 3. And they threw them in seven months, until the day when thou wast born: but thy mother hid thee three months; and they told about her. 4. And she made for thee an ark, and covered it with pitch and asphalt, and laid it in the grass, on the bank of the river, and placed thee into it seven days; and thy mother came in the night and nursed thee, and during the days thy sister Miriam protected thee from the wild animals. 5. And in those days Tarmuth, the daughter of Pharoah, came to bathe in the river, and she heard thy voice crying, and she told her Hebrew maidens that they should bring thee out; and they brought thee to them. 6. And they took thee out of the ark, and she pitied thee. 7. And thy sister said: "Shall I go and call for thee one of the Hebrew women, who shall raise and nurse this child for thee?" 8. And she said: "Go." 9. And she went and called thy mother Jokabed, and she gave her wages, and she raised thee. 10. And when thou didst grow, they brought thee to the house of Pharoah, and thou becamest his son; and Anbaram, thy father, taught thee writing. 11. And when thou didst complete three weeks, he brought thee to the royal court. 12. And thou wast in the court three weeks of years, until the day when thou didst go out of the royal court, and didst see the Egyptian as he was beating thy friend from among the children of Israel. 13. And thou slewest him and hid him in the sand, and on the following day thou foundest two of the children of Israel quarrelling, and didst say to the more powerful: "Why dost thou beat thy brother?" 14. And he became angry and wroth, and said: "Who has set thee a ruler and prince over us? 15. Dost thou desire to kill me, as thou didst kill the Egyptian yesterday?" 16. And thou didst fear and flee on account of these words.

CHAP. XLVIII. 1. And in the sixth year of the third week of the forty-ninth jubilee, thou didst go and dwell here five weeks and one year, and didst return to Egypt in the second week, in the second year, in the fiftieth jubilee. 2. And thou knowest what he spoke to thee at Mt. Sinai, and what the prince Mastema desired to do with thee, as thou returnest to Egypt, on the way, at the feast of tabernacles. 3. Did he not with all his power seek to kill thee, and to save the Egyptians out of thy hand, when thou sawest that thou wert sent to deliver judgments and vengeance over the Egyptians? 4. And I delivered thee out of his hands, and thou didst the signs and wonders for which I had sent thee to do in Egypt over Pharoah and over all his house and over his servants and over his people. 5. And the Lord inflicted a great vengeance upon them for Israel's sake, and beat them and killed them through blood and frogs and flies and dog flies and breaking-out skin-diseases, and also their animals by death, and through hail, by which he destroyed everything that grew for them; and through grasshoppers, who ate the rest that had been left by the hail, and through darkness; and also the first-born of man and animals; and on all their idols the Lord took vengeance and burned them with fire. 6. And everything was sent through thy hand, that thou shouldst do it before it was done, and thou didst tell it to the king of Egypt and before all of his servants and before his people. 7. And everything took place according to thy words: ten great and terrible judgments came over the land of Egypt, that they might take vengeance for Israel. And all the deeds of the Lord concerning Israel and according to his ordinance which he covenanted with Abraham, that he would take vengeance upon them, according as they had served the Egyptians in oppression. 8. And the prince Mastema placed himself against thee, and endeavored to throw thee into the hand of Pharoah and aided the sorcerers of the Egyptians, and stood by them, and they performed them before thee: the evils, however, we permitted them to perform, but their remedies we did not suffer them to perform by their hands. 9. And the Lord struck them with a dire pox, and they were not able to withstand, for we destroyed them so that they could not do a single sign. 10. And amid all the signs and wonders, the prince Mastema was not ashamed, until he became powerful and cried to the Egyptians that they should pursue after thee with all the power of the Egyptians, with their wagons and with their horses and with all the masses of the people of Egypt. 11. And I stood between the Egyptians and thee, and between them and Israel, and I saved the Israelites out of their hands and out of the hands of the Egyptians. 12. And the Lord led them through the middle of the sea, as if it were dry land. 13. And all the people he caused to come out to pursue Israel, the Lord our God cast into the midst of the sea, into the depths of the abysses, instead of the children of Israel, because the people of

Egypt had thrown their children by the hundreds into the river: vengeance was taken upon them and one thousand powerful men, and those that were strong, perished on account of one suckling babe which they had cast into the river from amongst thy people.   14. And on the fourteenth day, and on the fifteenth day, and on the sixteenth day, and on the seventeenth day, and on the eighteenth day, the prince Mastema was bound and chained behind the children of Israel, so that he could not accuse the children of Israel.   15. But on the nineteenth day we let him loose, so that he could help the Egyptians, and that they could pursue the children of Israel; and he made hard their hearts and strengthened them and he became powerful according to the Lord our God, so that he could smite the Egyptians and hurl them into the sea.   16. And on the fifteenth day we bound him, so that he could not accuse the children of Israel on the day when they asked for the utensils and clothing from the men of Egypt, utensils of silver and utensils of gold and utensils of iron, in order to despoil the Egyptians for having served him a service in oppression: and we did not cause the children of Israel to go out of Egypt empty-handed.

CHAP. XLIX.   1. Remember the command which the Lord commanded thee concerning the Pascah, that thou shalt keep it in its time, on the fourteenth of the first month, that thou shalt kill it before the evening come, and that they shall eat it during the night, on the evening of the fifteenth, from the time of the setting of the sun, for this is the first day of the festival and the first Pascah.   2. But ye were engaged in eating the Pascah in Egypt while all the powers of Mastema were sent forth in Egypt to destroy all the first-born in the land of Egypt, from the first-born of Pharoah to the first-born of the captive servant maid in the mill, and down to the animals.   3. And this is the sign which the Lord gave them: In every house at whose portals they had thrown the blood of a year old sheep, into this house they did not enter to kill those that were locked in it, so that all who were in the house were saved, because the sign of blood was upon the portals. 4. And the powers of the Lord did everything as the Lord commanded them, and they passed by all the sons of Israel, and no plague came over them to destroy any soul from their midst, neither of beast nor of man, not even a dog. And the plague was in Egypt exceedingly great, and there was no house in Egypt in which there was no dead body and weeping and lamentation.   5. And all Israel was engaged in eating the meat of the Pascah and drinking wine, and they lauded and thanked and blessed the Lord God of their fathers, and were prepared to go out from under the yoke of Egypt and from under its slavery. 6. But thou, remember this day all the days of thy life, once in the year, on its day, according to all the law thereof, and thou shalt not change the day for another day, or the month for another month. 7. For it is an ordinance of eternity, which is engraven on the tablets of heaven concerning the children of Israel, that they shall observe each year by year the festivals; once a year, in all their generations, and it has no limit of days, for it is ordained for eternity. 8. And a man, if he is pure and does not come to observe in its time the day, to bring an offering which is acceptable before the Lord on the day of the festival, and to eat and to drink before the Lord, on the day of his festival, that man shall be rooted out, if he is pure and near, because he has not brought the offering to the Lord in its time, on the fourteenth of the first month, between the evenings, in the third part of the day to the third part of the night; for two parts of the day are given to the light and the third to the evening; this it is that the Lord has commanded that thou shalt observe it between the evenings. 9. And it shall not take place in the morning, at any time of daylight, but only at the limits of the evenings; and they shall eat it in the time of evening until the third night, and whatever is left of all the meat on the third night, they shall again burn in the fire. 10. And they shall not cook it in water and shall not eat it raw, but carefully roasted on the fire and broiled on the fire; its head together with the intestines they shall roast, and its feet, and shall not break any bone within it, for none of the children of Israel shall have any bone broken. 11. On this account the Lord has commanded the children of Israel to observe the Pascah on the day of its time, and that no bone in it shall be broken, for it is a festival and a day commanded, and there must be no change from it from one day to another, or from one month to another, but on the day shall its festival be observed. 12. But thou, command the children of Israel that they should observe the Pascah on its days in all the years, once each year, on the day of its fixed time, and that it shall become a memorial before the Lord which is acceptable, and that no plague come over them to kill them and to scourge them in that year. 13. If they observe the Pascah in its time in everything as they have been commanded, then it is not allowed them to eat it outside of the sanctuary of the Lord, and all the people of the assembly of Israel shall observe it in its time. 14. Every man who is twenty years and above who comes on that day shall eat it in the sanctuary of your God before the Lord, for thus it is written and ordained that they shall eat it in the sanctuary of the Lord. 15. And when the children of Israel come into the land which they shall possess, into the land of Canaan, and plant the tent of the Lord in the midst of the land, within one of their hosts, until the time when the sanctuary of the Lord shall have been built in the land, then they shall come and observe the Pascah in the midst of the tent of the Lord, and shall sacrifice it before the Lord from year to year. 16. And in the days when a house shall have been built in the name of the Lord in the land of their inheritance, they shall go there and slay the Pascah in the evening, as the sun goes down, in the third part of the day. 17. And they shall place the blood on the foundation of the altar, and the fat they shall lay upon the fire upon the altar, and shall eat flesh thereof that has been roasted at the fire, in the court of the sanctuary in the name of the Lord. 18. And they must not observe the Pascah in their cities and in all their districts, but only before the tent of the Lord or before his house, where his name dwells, so that ye do not trespass against the Lord. 19. But thou, Moses, command the children of Israel, that they shall observe the ordinance of the Pascah as it has been commanded to thee, that they shall observe the day year by year, and its day and the festival of the unleavened bread, that they shall eat unleavened bread seven days, so that they observe its festival, that they bring an offering day by day in these seven days of the Pascah before the Lord on the altar of your God. 20. For this festival ye observed with trembling when ye went out of Egypt until ye had gone through the sea into the desert of Sur, for on the shore of the sea ye completed it.

CHAP. L. 1. And after this law I made known to thee the days of Sabbaths in the desert Sinai, which is between Elam and Sinai. 2. And I told you concerning the Sabbaths of the earth on Mt. Sinai, and concerning the years of jubilees with the Sabbaths; and also the year I mentioned to you; but the year thereof we did not tell you, until thou comest into the land which ye shall possess; and ye shall make the land also observe the Sabbaths for those dwelling in it, and the years of jubilees shall learn. 3. Concerning this I have ordained for thee the weeks of years and the jubilees, from the days of Adam to this day: forty-nine (jubilees) and one week and two years; and yet forty years are before for learning the commandments of the Lord, until ye cross the border of the land of Canaan, crossing the Jordan on the western side, and jubilees will pass by until Israel shall be cleansed from all fornication and guilt and uncleanness and contamination and sin and transgression, and shall dwell in all the land in safety, and no Satan and no evil one will injure him, and the land will be cleansed from that time on and to eternity. 4. And, behold, the command of the Sabbaths I have written down for thee, and all the judgments of its laws. 5. Six days thou shalt do work, and on the seventh day is the Sabbath of the Lord, your God; ye shall not do any work on it, neither ye, nor your children, nor your male servants, nor your maid servants, nor any of your beasts, nor your stranger who is with you. 6. The man that does any work on it shall die, and every man who descrates this day, who lies with a wife, and who says that he will do something on it, that he will make a trip on it, or concerning all buying and selling, and who draws water on it which he did not prepare for himself on the sixth day, and whoever takes up a burden to carry it out of his tent or out of his house, he shall die. 7. Ye shall not do any work on the Sabbath which ye have not prepared for yourselves on the sixth day, to eat or to drink or to rest or to keep Sabbath from all your work on that day, and to bless the Lord your God, who has given it to you as a festival day; and a holy day it shall be, and a day of the holy kingdom, for all Israel this day, among your days, in all the days. 8. For great is the honor which the Lord has given to Israel to eat and to drink and to be satisfied on this festival day, after resting on this day from all the work of the children of men, except burning frankicense and bringing offerings and sacrifices before the Lord on the days and the Sabbaths. 9. This work alone shall be done on the Sabbath days, in the sanctuary of the Lord your God, so that these shall appear over Israel as a constant atonement, day by day, as a memorial, which is acceptable before the Lord and received forever, day by day, as I have command-ed thee. 10. And every man who does any work on this day, or makes a journey, or works his land, be it in the house or at any other place, and whoever lights a fire or rides upon any beast, or travels by ship upon the sea, and everyone that strikes or kills anything, or kills an animal or a bird, and who catches an animal and bird and fish, and who contends or engages in war on the Sabbath day, shall die, so that the children of Israel shall observe the Sabbaths, according to the command of the Sabbath of the land, as it is written on the tablets of heaven, which he gave into my hands, that I should write for thee the laws of the times, and the different times in the division of their days.